The Humanics Elleesium Declaration 2019

London: On April 06: 2019

The Humanicsxian Manifesto

Munayem Mayenin

An Imsonium Book

Dedication

Let this work invite the world's working humanity to remember The Tolpuddle Martyrs, a group of six agricultural workers, from Dorset, England in the 19th century, who stood and fought and were punished for daring to seek to advance workers' rights: James Brine, James Hammett, George Loveless, James Loveless, Thomas Standfield and John Standfield

---

Dehumanisation of Humanity

This work is based on this fundamental

People are free because they are equal and they are equal because they are free. Without equality in existence liberty cannot exist, and without liberty in existence equality cannot either. This is the rationale, in which a new civilisation must be born to replace this uncivilised, ruthless and brutal system of so called civilisation; that is based on power, rooted in money, owning, winning and pride, that is expressed and exercised in the fiercest of competition and, that is run like an excellent machine, and that tries to put the mask of ration in the ugliest of irrationality and, that waters and nurtures inhumanity and bars all the avenues of human potentials to be-to be free and equal and to live and deny to accept a state of merely staying alive.

Munayem Mayenin
London
2004

''If, you believe in Humanics you are a humanicsxian or humanictian: hu:ma:nic:tian, so that you aspire to think in new ways, anew, afresh, you aspire to be and do in a new way and in that new way of thinking, being, doing, working, creating and existing, you aspire to live your life in Human Enterprise, which is an idea arising out of Humanics in which no one owns anything but everyone belongs to the whole as the whole belongs to everyone lawfully and equally and, it neither believes in nor makes money but human utilities, needs, aspirations, creativity, imagination and dreams are served without money, where everyone works and creates for others as others create and work for them, thus, bringing in meaning and purpose to life along with it come natural justice, equality and liberty that establish a true civilisation.''

Humanics: The Foundation: Munayem Mayenin: Published: December 06: 2017

The Humanicsxian Compact

One World's One Working Humanity Unite Organise And Rise As One

Karl Marx was the first philosopher to teach us some fundamentals: a: that it is Philosophy, that we need and, that, it, Philosophy, needs not only to seek to try and explain the world but change it, b: that the world is ONE with all her problems and prospects, c: that this world, therefore, must UNITE to secure change, d: that change happens by the 'powerfuls' for their own vested interests and benefits, while subjugating most others, ensuring a life of absolute, rotten and cruel indignity, hardship and suffering for them and their future generations, unless REVOLUTIONARIES UNITE and INITIATE a change, that is beneficial to all, e: that there is no other way of achieving 'positive' change but that we seek and strive as determinedly, as resolutely, as absolutely, as possible to achieve it. And from here we, must, take our first step and go forward: that history is not a living organism and it is neither a product of hatred nor of class struggle; rather, it is that, what we seek to make it; if, we do not take part in the making of it, it is going to serve only those, who want to dominate the majority. If, we do not have any power, as we don't, for most people are absolutely powerless against the system's almost-infinite' prowess, than the history shall continue to be made by people like Bonaparte, like Hitler, by despots and dictators and by those, who pretend and spend millions to make people believe that they are 'people's champions. If, on the other hand, we take the view, that it is us, the humanion, as the metaphorical physiology of the entire humanity, where each individual human being is and behaves and acts like a cell does in a body: always, working together with other cells, not working against each other, in unison to achieve continuous homeostasis, harmony, sustenance and progression of life and the human condition, who make history, than, we, must, take charge of making history, than, we, must, but this we start with an I, stand up to the mark and go about making and shaping that history.

And this is how this goes: there are nine steps between imagination and reality: i: imagination, ii: prospectivity, iii: tentativity, iv: feasibility, v: possibility, vi: onwardineity, vii: probability, viii: certainty and ix: reality; these are the nine-step-realm-path of reality, through which, human endeavours begin and progress towards reality. And in none of these nine realms, at no time, at no place, at no space, there is either a space or a case for hatred, bloodshed and violence; rather, continual learning and development, knowledge and wisdom, must, always, be our fireflies to guide us through. And in this path, HISTORY, must, never be, let to imprison us, dictate us, manipulate us, set the terms and protocols of our endeavours for we are not seeking to live in the past nor are we striving to recreate the dreams:nightmares of others from the past but to materialise our own dreams, visions and ideals to make our own history. It is mammoth of a symphonic work: a symphonic piece of work can not produce a symphony, if, it seeks to achieve it through hatred, bloodshed and violence.

Let us imagine, natural justice, built on liberty and equality on the grounds of law and due process of law, where Humanicsovics, a direct form of humanical democracy, not representative democracy, in which each and every human individual is his:her own High Representative, flowers; feeding our humanity throughout the humanion, that lives in the bodies and minds of, each and every single individual, all individual persons of the humanion. And on this path, let us be on guard that no country, which is a village, no nation, which is a geo-located humanity, no map, which is a drawn-up piece of paper, no colour, which is a geo-thermal-biologico-genetic-jacket for humanity, that is to enable it to respond to evolutionary and environmental changed realities, because humanity is colourless in its mind:soul:will, no language, which is a means of thinking, creation, discourse, study and communications, no religion, which is an expression of faith, no status, which is imposed, no gender, which is a duo-natural-expression of humanity, no passport, a wee-book of printed papers and no history, which, so far, has been manipulated by the powerfuls to impose their wills, prowess and dictatorship to the majority of humanity, no hatred, for it is anti-ration, anti-reason, anti-science, anti-mathematics, anti-logic, anti-ethics, anti-morality, anti-nature and anti-humanity, no prejudice, which is a germ of ignorance, no violence and bloodshed, for these two are the duo-slaughterer of reason, love, faith, hope, compassion, mercy and humanity and no FRONTIER, for there is none in the human physiology and none in the human mind and none there is in nature and in the entire spread of the Mother Universana, divide us from being and becoming a humanion on this Earth and on this Mother Universana: with humanity, care, compassion, respect, love, enlightenment, humanionship and wisdom in a soul-commune-ecology-of-humanity, created, sustained and strengthened by our kinships, by our bonds, by our connections, by our oneness, by our diversities, by our actions, interactions and inter-exchanges, by our myriad of different types of human relationships, friendships and by our political, economical, learning and developmental, social, cultural, artistic and spiritual engagements, celebrations and enjoyment of life and existence in our persons, families and communities in all areas, arenas, fields, sectors, spheres and domains of life and existence on this earth.

The working humanity of the world, the vast, vast, vast, majority of humanion, who are the only and the sole and the astonishing magicians, who are able to and who can and do utilise their infinities of imagination, creativity and ingenuity, that constitute humanity and create every worth, every value and every wealth on this earth, that all, capitalism enables the rich to steal, rob and use and abuse by sentencing the entire working humanity to a live-in-life-sentence of serving all high-cruelties in brutal, barbaric and vicious hardship, suffering, agony and pain. Let the one world's working humanity organise, unite and rise as one in each country, in each nation and in each and every people on earth and create a universal grid of an organised political and philosophical symphony of risen working humanity, working together in one purpose, in one aim, in one goal, in one destination, bound for and to one and the same destiny: to eradicate the monstrosities, high-cruelties and barbarities of the killing-mechanism capitalism and to create and establish a humanical civilisation, a humanical society, on earth for all humanity, eradicating ownership and money and replacing that with belongingship, where everything, the whole belongs to everyone and all belongs to the whole at all times equally under the law, where the public affairs management system is conducted under humanicsovics, where the political economics, business, trade and commerce are conducted in human enterprise, setting the entire humankind free at equality and liberty, under the rule of law, in natural justice, where humanity is set free on the path of eternal and continual learning, development and progression. In humanics humanity becomes an infinity unfolding itself: being at liberty and equality, living for a purpose in life and existence and being, doing and creating for a meaning, whereby everyone works for others while all others do the same so that, for the first time, since the dawn of humanity, selflessness and giving eradicate and replace selfishness for every single human being exists to create and give all her:his creations for the benefits of the rest of humanity while the entire humanity does the same. There, in such a humanical society, everyone's needs, necessities and utilities are met by the works and creations of others and because in such society the entire capable and willing human beings are working to produce the highest possible amount of economic and creative output, that can and will be able to meet all human needs. Therefore, The Humanics Elleesium Declaration 2019, The Humanicsxian Manifesto calls upon the entire working humanity of the entire world and the entire humankind to organise, unite and rise as one to strive to seek to try: to do: to change: to make better the human condition in humanics. One world's One Working Humanity Unite, Organise And Rise As One.

The Humanics Elleesium Declaration 2019

Humanity will continue to live an inferior life than what is possible until the two halves, women and men, with all individuals in them, are absolutely, fundamentally and jubilantly equal at liberty. Humanity, therefore, is not and can not be free until all humans are equals for only by the yardstick of this equality their state of being free can be measured. In other words, there can not exist liberty unless there exists equality between and among all humans and this state of equality can not come to exist so long there remain two groups of humans: the powerful and the powerless: whereby the former controls the later and creates, maintains and carries forward the perpetual state of inequality: economically, politically, judicially, constitutionally, socially, culturally and spiritually. To reach the state of equality and liberty, the task before humanity is, therefore, to change this state by taking away ownership and money and, with them, the power they generate and confer, that lets one small group of humans, the powerfuls, subjugating the vast multitude of humans, the powerless, under their dictatorship. For only by taking away 'the gun' of the power of the powerfuls, humanity can bring about the state of liberty, as well as, equality at once: equality and liberty can not and do not exist separately but together and simultaneously. Equality and liberty exist as the Promethumean fire: in which there is the light and there is the heat in one flame: the humanion stands here on the path of humanics: a state of liberty for all humanity at equality. The Promethumean: where Prometheus is not seen as a man but a human. In such a humanical society all humans are, for the first time, in human history of progression, set free at liberty and at equality for there remain no powerfuls, who derive their power from ownership and from their possession of money and wealth and, thus, there remain no powerless for no one has any power to dominate others under their prowess.

The Humanics Elleesium Declaration 2019

The Humanicsxian Manifesto

The Humanics Elleesium Declaration 2019

The Humanicsxian Manifesto

Munayem Mayenin, London, United Kingdom

ISBN: 978-0-244-76474-6

Copyrights @ Munayem Mayenin, London, UK
First Published: April 06: 2019
Price: £05.00
An Imsonium Book

The Humanics Elleesium Declaration 2019

To state the existential imperative of humanity in a world, that has neither a body nor a philosophy, that will enable it to create a system of governance of the public affairs management, political economics and jurisprudence, that support, sustain, enhance, foster and nurture the human condition in a civic society under the rule of law in natural justice, where equity and fairness guide all the persons of humanity and all the agencies, that humanity creates and runs, in which, humanity can exist as humanity-naturale: that all humans are equal and that they all are at liberty at all times and all spheres of existence while they all are educated to the highest degree possible and they all are engaged in eternal learning so to keep their infinite imagination, creativity and ingenuity on the path of eternal progress and development, is to say that it has no alternative but to gather itself together around a new philosophy, new political philosophy, new political economics, new jurisprudence and new sociology and rise to challenge, fight and defeat the monstrosities and high-cruelties, including, poverty of all kinds, manners and forms, inequalities, hunger and homelessness, that capitalism distributes and in so doing creates sociological squalors in societies, that establish the sociology of evil by the implementation of dehumanisation, fragmentation, isolation, dismantling, disabling, disconnecting, disenfranchising and disempowering humanity, which are imposed and established with a vicious and ruthless war of dehumanisation of humanity against humanity, conducted and implemented by the distorteddia conglomerate to the vast majority of humanity and this rise to challenge, fight and defeat the current horrendous capitalistic onslaught on human existence must be conducted with a determination to establish a humanical society of humanity on earth, that will eradicate ownership and money and replace them with belongingship, in which all the economic and political economical affairs are conducted in human enterprise whereby no person nor group nor groups of persons nor any agency nor group of agencies nor consortium nor consortia of them nor states nor governments nor any other type of agencies or entities own anything. The very concept of ownership has been eliminated and it does not exist any longer.

Humanity will continue to live an inferior life than what is possible until the two halves, women and men, with all individuals in them, are absolutely, fundamentally and jubilantly equal at liberty. Humanity, therefore, is not and can not be free until all humans are equals for only by the yardstick of this equality their state of being free can be measured. In other words, there can not exist liberty unless there exists equality between and among all humans and this state of equality can not come to exist so long there remain two groups of humans: the powerful and the powerless: whereby the former controls the later and creates, maintains and carries forward the perpetual state of inequality: economically, politically, judicially, constitutionally, socially, culturally and spiritually. To reach the state of equality and liberty, the task before humanity is, therefore, to change this state by taking away ownership and money and, with them, the power they generate and confer, that lets one small group of humans, the powerfuls, subjugating the vast multitude of humans, the powerless, under their dictatorship. For only by taking away 'the gun' of the power of the powerfuls, humanity can bring about the state of liberty, as well as, equality at once: equality and liberty can not and do not exist separately but together and simultaneously. Equality and liberty exist as the Promethumean fire: in which there is the light and there is the heat in one flame: the humanion stands here on the path of humanics in human enterprise, working to establish a humanical society: a state of liberty for all humanity at equality. The Promethumean is used here where Prometheus is not seen as a man but a human. In such a humanical society all humans are, for the first time, in human history of progression, set free at liberty and at equality for there remain no powerfuls, who derive their power from ownership and from their possession of money and wealth and, thus, there remain no powerless for no one has any power to dominate others under their prowess.

A humanical society creates the conditions of production and distribution of all the created goods, services and provisions to the highest possible level and degree because that society employs the highest possible number of its citizens; those, who are able to work and who are willing to work are employed in all economical activities. All the created products, services and provisions are, then, distributed to the centres of distributions, using all the existing networks of routes and logistics, in all places, villages, towns, cities and communities from where people take whatever they need and everyone works in the field, in which one has developed expertise. A teacher teaches while a surgeon operates, a solicitor represents a client while a social worker serves her case-loads, as farmers produce farming produce as other workers catch and bring fish to the markets but everyone's needs are met without any payment because there no longer exists money nor there exists any manufactured and artificial need for money. This system of political economics is called human enterprise, that is not run by political party system nor is it run by an elite but by a direct form of democracy, humanicsovics. Humanicsovics is run by individual citizens, working together in a constitutionally organised and architectured manner and mechanism. Pre-humanical societies will still be run by party political system so to seek to bring capitalism under the rule of law and employ it to work to create, deliver and prepare humanity towards the development, creation and ushering in of humanical societies. In a humanical society the state and government, legislature and judiciary still exist but their organisation, the structure, the running and maintenance and their conduct and functioning change because of humanicsovics, a direct humanical form of democracy, so that they appear not as how we define and see these bodies as but, as, if, they had gone through a metamorphosis and out of which, for the first time in the history of human development, society has finally, developed its own mechanism to conduct itself within the rule of law in natural justice. In this, in humanical society, the states and their governments and the legislatures and the judiciaries, the public administration, civic and community services are all 'structures', that are owned and guided and run by society itself as its individual members of humanity are working together and directly running the public affairs management system through humanicsovics, that is not conducted by or through political parties. Therefore, Karl Marx's prediction that in communism states will simply wither away can be rephrased as this: that in humanical societies they will not wither away but go through a metamorphosis and rise as restructured and re-organised and re-orientated organisations of society itself, that enables all its members to have the degree of education and learning to acquire the knowledge, skills, qualities, characteristics, aptitudes and competencies, that are necessary to be able to carry out and conduct the running, development and maintenance of these bodies, that belong to society and all its members or citizens. In this, humanical societies will have no state nor government the way they exist today. The pre-humanical society will have created the conditions for these bodies, the states and governments, to go through the metamorphosis and become re-casted into becoming bodies and organisations of society itself, that are run directly by the members of that society: by individuals, working together without any political crowd-pulling or 'party whipping' for they conduct themselves as mathematicians or as scientists. They do not argue nor do they opinioneer but they discuss and debate as rational minds and agree quickly when a solution is found and they are not controlled by party political dogma nor interests nor are they controlled by any other forces or interest or interest groups.

The human condition has not hitherto seen such most vicious, most fierce, most cruel, most barbaric and most doggedly determined brutal and continuous philosophical, political philosophical, political economical, jurisprudential and socio-cultural war being lodged and conducted against it, through the ultimate globalised spread and setting-up of capitalism, supported by a ruthlessly self-serving distorteddia conglomerate, both, together, have, successfully, taken over the states and their governments, regardless of what political forces run them and imposed a Distorteddia Lordship over the populace and entangled both the people as individuals, as families, as communities, as organisations and all the agencies of all manners and types, that people create and run. Despite the unprecedented advancement in learning, knowledge-advancing achievements, in all branches of sciences, medicine, mathematics, engineering and research, innovation and ingenuity and the unimaginable strides, that have been taken in technological advancements and the development of systems, mechanisms, apparatus, networks or the architecture to create, support, sustain, nurture, foster and advance a far superior, far sophisticated and far humanity-nurturing human existence, yet, the vast multitude of humanity across the world are sentenced to serve all high-cruelties in a live-in-life-sentence of misery, suffering, agony and pain, in which, humanity is getting mauled, devastated and torn apart in receiving the vicious and barbaric onslaught of all these high-cruelties: hunger, malnutrition, severe and acute malnutrition, semi-hunger, perpetual hunger, working poverty, unemployment, unemployability, homelessness, rough-sleeping, destitution, beggary, no-education, no-medication, illnesses, no social security protection, no pension, no social care and, added to all this, further high-cruelties are imposed on these humanity through lack of clean and safe water to drink, lack of safe and clean toilets and hygiene and personal health provisions, as well as, lack of clean and healthy environment and lack of clean, pure and natural air to breathe. Yet, despite all this progress in all these fields, areas, arenas and spheres of life, the resultants have been 'robbed' off by the rich and, in turn, the rich are harvesting the proceeds while education has been pushed down, even, lower than the 'any other business' part of the agenda and life-long learning does not have any meaning whatsoever other than getting 'lip service'. In all countries, from the least developed to the highly developed, higher education has been turned into a debt-bondage and despite the highest development in education provisions in the higher education sector these institutions are shut to the majority. Furthermore, the 'token' mandatory education up to the age of 16 have been made into a 'factory', particularly, in the advanced economy countries, where the states are spending less and less resources so that the young people are supposed to just 'go through' the years without much expectations or achievements and, consequently, a vast majority of these young people are leaving their last statutory schools without having acquired the ability to read or write or add or subtract. Therefore, they leave the statutory education by, effectively, becoming 'unemployable'. In short, the absolute incongruity and paradox of this capitalist system can be seen in the juxtaposition of these two sharply contrasting realities: that the highest most of development in almost all areas of human existence has created the highest possible economic output with which humanity could create, support, nurture, foster and advance the human condition to an unimaginable state and the entire human kind could be supported to reach for and get educated to the highest possible level while the small club of the rich pocket these entire economic output and sentence the populace with all the high-cruelties where the human condition keeps going backwards: hunger is increasing, poverty is increasing, inequality is increasing, education is walking backward, life-long learning has no legs to walk and arisen out of these desperations working poverty, child poverty, poverty for people with disabilities, poverty for people, who are elderly, frail and ill, poverty for pensioners, poverty for younger generation, poverty for people with mental illness and poverty for minorities of all kinds and poverty for indigenous peoples of the world. In other words: as opposed to being humanity-naturale, due to facing these ever-going onslaught of war of dehumanisation by the capitalist apparatus and its entire 'army' of the distorteddia conglomerate, humanity faces a seize by the sociology of evil in rapidly advancing sociology of squalor where the human condition has been made and, increasingly, being made, into a 'punishment' of a live-in-life-sentence of suffering and perishing away by the continual chopping by all these enforced high-cruelties, that arise out of poverty, inequality, disempowerment, fragmentation, disconnection, isolation and disenfranchisement of all kinds, types and manners.

In our critique of the collapse of socialist experimentations and the globalised capitalism's re-assertion and re-establishment as 'the political economical system', Dehumanisation of Humanity', we have shown as to why and how the socialistic experimentation failed and fell away, falling back onto the lap of capitalism despite some countries still calling themselves socialist or communist countries while enforcing their 'order' through the old communist party style of manners. In many countries in the world there are political parties, some call themselves socialist, some communist, some social democratic, some national socialist, some workers' parties etc but no one can run a socialist economy in a world, that speaks capitalism because the entire architecture to conduct business, trade and commerce and all economic endeavours are capitalistic so that capitalism has achieved its ultimate prowess. However, following the falling apart of the socialist block of countries created a 'disequilibrium' in the world stage whereby the balance has been broken and, that offers the advanced capitalistic countries to take advantage for this sudden lack of balance. In this disequilibrium USA is seeking to monopolise the world while other countries are rising to challenge that and stake their case, such as, Russia, China, India, Brazil and so on. However, what, effectively, happened is this that this destroyed the internationalism in all political parties. Now, no political party has any international dimension any longer. All political parties are now functioning without relation to or regard to world affairs, state of the world and the destiny of the people of the world. In this newly-developed and deteriorating world situation, the United Nations have been falling apart and becoming a 'paper tiger' while 'isolationism', various types of raw and crass nationalism and self-interest seeking tendencies have been advancing. Wars, conflicts and foreign interventions in countries have increased and various world powers have taken sides in these wars and conflicts, thus, fuelling them; however, these wars and conflicts not only created mass graveyards for slaughtered human lives but, also, uprooted hundreds of millions of people and set them out onto the savage roads to go and find safety, which have been reaching other countries and creating havoc of problems in them. Added to this, a great number of countries in many parts of the world, where wars and conflicts devastated their states, that caused a devastating falling apart of infrastructures and people are running out of their countries in search of work and food and for better life and these hundreds of millions of people are running towards the economically better countries, where they are creating further problems. All these massive displacements and movements of people stand to challenge the existing systems and apparatus of these countries, that are finding it difficult to deal with these problems. Added to this is the rise of all the extreme, racist, xenophobic and white supremacist forces, that are using these to advance their neo-nazism and neo-fascism in a cocktail of white supremacy and nationalism blended into a deadly mix. These forces are advancing in many countries in the world, where there are varying degrees of extremisations, where nasty and reactionary forces are using religion and other identities, including, clans and other groupings, to their armoury and arsenals.

Added to these calamitous scenarios the capitalistic consumerism has reached a point whereby the very dangerous ways in which consumptions take place devastate the environment and the conditions and ecology of life and devastate all the variables in the web of life on earth. This created the existential dangers to humanity because the capitalist consumerist culture without regards to their consequences caused climate change and global warming, that are threatening the existence of human communities in many parts of the worlds because of increased and more ferocious expressions of floods, cyclones, tornadoes, tsunamis, heat waves and cold waves whereby heat waves reaching higher and cold waves going lower and rains are either becoming less and weak or becoming heavy and more while droughts are becoming harsher and more devastating, all these are creating hostile and inhospitable conditions for human communities to be able to continue existence there so that massive number of people, entire communities are forced to move away, searching for newer places to live in. While other places, global warming has caused sea level to rise, threatening the very existence of island nations and communities and they are left without a future in their own islands, yet, they had nowhere else to go nor do they have any recourse to correct the threats imposed by the risen sea level while they still face harsher and harder expressions of more and frequent natural disasters. In many parts of the world, particularly, the Caribbean islands, face an unprecedented occurrence of natural disasters, in such magnitude and such violent ferocity that in the last bout of tornadoes and hurricanes, many of these island nations have lost most of their infrastructures, entirely wiped out into a landscape of absolute devastations to which they look on without any clue as to how to rebuild all that loss and, all of them are wondering as to what, if, then, these new built are demolished once again? All these are impacting on colossal level and degree of further changes and devastations in all surfaces of the earth, the land, the ocean, the air. The environment has become dangerously unhealthy, the water bodies have been devastated by global warming and climate change but they are, further, devastated by the import of plastic, micro and nano plastic pollution, as well as, other chemical pollution in industrial areas. Human lives and condition are far more devastated by the polluted air by which many human lives are being lost, in addition to this, hundreds of millions of people, who are ill, elderly and frail and suffering from vary many health conditions, including, new-borns, babies, toddlers and infants are suffering the terrible and life-changing devastations because of breathing in toxic and polluted air. The world is incapable of dealing with any of these issues because it has no body of its own to work as one to deal with these existential threats to humanity.

In short, the world does not exist as a unity, there are countries and there are peoples and there are nations, in which, humanity has neither a home nor a destination. The entire world stage seems to offer validation to William Shakespeare's metaphor of the world being a stage: on it everyone is 'strutting and fretting' without anything to put forward other than the submission to capitalism and its newest invention and ally: the distorteddia conglomerate, both of which, have been working together to conduct this vicious and continuous war of dehumanisation of humanity and life and human existence across the world have been made into a 'dog-eat-dog' world, a cruel and barbaric reality. In the advanced world these brutalities and sociological squalors, United States of America will be a leader in in this, are manifested in the massive and endemic devaluation of human lives, in which illicit and recreational and addictional drug use and abuse, is killing a huge number of the population and causing the rest, who are not dead yet, to have a semi-human quality of existence, in which they are simply waiting to succumb to death 'anytime soon', suffering from many illnesses and health conditions. In many such countries, again, USA leads the world in this, guns are slaughtering many lives and gun related crimes and homicides are increasing all the time, as well as, other necessary conditions of the sociological squalors and the sociology of evil are manifested in much crimes, gun crimes, knife crimes, acid being used as lethal weapons, gangs and gang-land culture, harassment, physical and verbal abuse, misogynistic and chauvinistic advancement, xenophobia and white supremacy and all other types of discriminatory agendas, hatred, prejudice and phobias are advancing, as well as, the natural social norm of conduct and behaviours have been deteriorating so that harassment, sexual harassment, sexual aggression and sexual abuse are becoming more and more everyday occurrence.

All the advancements made in relation to advancing workers' rights and bettering working conditions and citizens rights, civil liberties and human rights, woman's rights, anti-discriminatory practices, everything has been falling away and the human condition is pushed backward, further and further backward we keep on going. In this the rich are getting richer, the distorteddia conglomerate and all their contrapediums are being used to dehumanise people and in these robbery-fields of life and existence, statistics speak of horror of a human condition where millions of babies, toddlers, infants and children are dying of hunger and malnutrition, severe and acute malnutrition. Millions are dying of very many illnesses every year, that are easily preventable. Wars and conflicts in many places on earth are killing hundreds of thousands of humans, including, the most innocent, the children and making thousands and thousands disabled for life and, along with these devastations of humanity, hundreds of millions of people are uprooted from their homes and are left on the routes to roam the world, that does not give a toss about them and along these paths, human traffickers and others seeking to use them to make money as their victims, these desperate humanity keep on dying on routes, in the deserts or drowning in the seas, which are bringing slavery and slave markets back into reality in this horror of a world. The world simply stands as a graveyard for most human beings to keep on suffering and dying away. A sub-human existence is 'sentenced' to hundreds of millions of human beings, who are forced to suffer and perish away in the world's countless shanty towns, that are absolutely inhabitable for human beings. The fact that there are few billions of humans in this world is made a 'coping mechanism' so that it does not, even, make news that few million children die each year from easily preventable illnesses and diseases! But those, who do not die are the worse off for their live-in-life-sentence goes on and they remain suffering the consequences of all the high-cruelties, that capitalism imposes on people across the world. The nature of poverty is the same but expressions of it are different depending on what parts of the world one is looking at. However, now, capitalism has established its own narrative for which there are much propaganda; yet, the reality and the fact is this that: capitalism creates, maintains, sustains and distributes poverty, inequality, disenfranchisement and disempowerment, all of which, deliver to the majority of humanity all the high-cruelties: that people pay in two ways: one, through and in their own personal life and, the second, through experiencing the sociological squalor capitalism has created in the wider society where everything is falling apart for states and governments have been paying homage to their rich masters so that they are cutting severely on spending and investments in areas of public, civic and communal services and facilities; all that savage cuts create these sociology of squalors in which the sociology of evil thrives, that can be seen in the sociological squalor countries have been creating so that poverty has many dimensions: one is poor so that one lives in an area where there exists a sociological squalor, that shows how the sociology of evil is taking over existence. This is how dehumanisation has spread and continued to impact all landscapes, in which, humanity must exist.

Let us take a look at the dehumanisation of humanity a little more deeply: once, the virtues, characteristics, properties, states, straits, qualities, that constitute humanity, are taken down or are stripped off humanity, it becomes the exact opposite of what it is as humanity-naturale. Dehumanisation creates the sociology of evil through the establishment of sociological squalor, that demonstrates all kinds of poverty, inequality, disenfranchisement and disempowerment. The more dehumanisation advances the more humanity goes closer towards the sociology of evil, that creates and supports a jingoistic jungle, because that society follows a jingoistic political philosophy and jingoistic political economics, instead of a civic society and the more sociology of evil is increased the more it rages and savages humanity with its prowess. Sociology of evil is comprised of all the negative virtues, characteristics, properties, states, straits and qualities of humanity; once, each of these is erased or made to fall away from humanity, the physiology of humanity, then, falls to the negative of the same state: care falls to carelessness, love falls to hatred, compassion falls to selfishness, kindness falls to cruelty, understanding falls to intolerance, compassion falls to indifference, hope is replaced by cynicism and so on. A society, that is civic, is run under the rule of law, in natural justice, where everything supports the fostering and maintenance of all human virtues so that in such society humans are likely to love learning, to abide by the rule of law, to be civic minded, to be kind and considerate, to be loving and compassionate and so on. While people are dehumanised these human virtues, characteristics, properties, states, straits have no food to keep on going so that because of the 'hunger' humanity loses these virtues and the 'gap or void' is taken over by the negative states, that are part of the sociology of evil. A society, that creates sociological squalor because it has established poverty and inequality, that make people disenfranchised and disempowered so that everything has been cut and made short and bare so that localities have nothing for people, everything is falling apart and getting in disrepair and dilapidation. Sociology of evil creates sociological squalor and these keep on dehumanisations of all kinds going so that humanity keeps on getting strangled by the sheer power of the sociological squalor and its evils. The Houses of Parliament in the UK is a magnificent building and despite their political parties and affiliations all the members of these houses are better off than ordinary people for they earn big salaries for their job. They sit in this magnificent building and outside it, around the hidden passages and pathways, underground spaces, homeless people rough sleep and people go to work, walking passed or walking over them and, sometimes, they do so with dead bodies of rough sleepers, laying there on the pavements, These scenes show how wide this sociological squalor has reached in the UK and these sociological squalors exist in all countries, regardless of whether they are in advanced or least developed group of countries. If, one walks in central London for two hours, just following any road and going round and round, one would find hundreds and hundreds of homeless people, rough sleeping on wherever there is space for people to sit or sleep. But there are many other expressions of this sociology of squalor: many neighbourhoods show the devastations of this squalor: everything is falling apart, everything is getting shut and shuttered, dirty and unclean, broken down and dusty and debris-strewn. Shops are closed. Centres of any sort are closed, old facilities, old amenities are closing. Youth centres closed. Family centres closed. Sociology of squalor shows one thing: humanity is done here. Move away. Go somewhere else. Here resides sociology of evil in this sociological squalor. There are shops selling cheap things and there are food shops selling cheap and unhealthy food and people can only shop there by as much little money they have. They pay for their live-in-life-sentence and they get all soft of illnesses and they suffer and they die lot earlier than their rich counter parts. Everything is 'sentenced' here in this sociological squalor under the reign of the sociology of evil. Here much crime directs existence, much violence and wasted blood and spread out negations circulate the ecology of dehumanisation. Gangs spring up, ganglands advance, knives and guns make their hidden passages felt, drugs creep in and begin their devastations, alcoholism and all other abuse of all kinds and manners begin to enter the arenas, where humanity should exist. Here everything festers and produces that what kills: hatred and phobia, cynicism and loss of hope and enthusiasm are generated from all the miseries suffered. In this toxic ecology desperations make people more desperate and they subscribe to all forms and manners of presentations made by obnoxious forces to advance their horror-agenda and the distorteddia have disconnected the world and people with opinion fascism, dangerous and malicious falsehoods, fabrications, mythologies, lies and propaganda and with all these weapons the distorteddia conglomerate are directing, herding and manipulating people and advancing and supporting the spread of all forms and manners of filthy extreme reactionary forces while they make a killing out of the people using them.

Capitalism has used the development of technology into a weapon to advance technological dehumanisation and created and have been using the distorteddia or the distorteddia conglomerate, that are made of all the entities, that call themselves 'social media and this and the other, including, the entire jungle of the so called apps, gadgets, contraptions and platforms. There is something, profoundly dehumanising, deeply contradictory and, fundamentally, anti-nature is happening in society, that has been losing its power to the distorteddia or the entire range of distortive, fragmentary and, often, manipulative 'expressions of realities', that are, simply, seeking to mimic the reality and real society: except, these have neither reality nor society in them, whereby people are, simply, taken on the terms and basis of absolute and must dehumanisation. The market has established its grip so that we are herded to one place and are given 'scripts' by which to 'waste away' by, by, simply, being the 'consumers', buying and consuming, while ensuring that we become and remain nothing but a mob and that we are always at the herding place so that the market and the marketeers have everyone at their disposal, when they advertise their offerings and, along the way, save a great deal of money and make a hell of a killing from it.

These distorteddia have been let to grow because the entire 'mechanism' from the states and governments to media and publications to universities and businesses and all other from all spheres and all parts of the world, simply, let everything being dragged along and with such a naive, unquestioning, submissive and bedazzled way, that these agencies of the entire world had offered the best and highest most validation, prestige and recommendations, as well as, free advertisements to these distorteddia conglomerate and with it they amassed vast number of human beings just falling into their nets and the more fell the more billions they made and, now, things are becoming insanely obvious as to how desperately dangerous this is getting. It is time to wake up and do something about it. These distorteddia are the most dangerous development in the human progression but these are more dangerous than just physical annihilation of humanity for these are slaughtering the very humanity we are supposed to be and turning us into a mob.

People have been, increasingly, becoming nothing more or nothing less than, only, good enough for being part of the mob and staying as such at the herding place, photographed, videoed themselves doing nothing and then self-broadcast these goings on of doing and being nothing. People have no other value or virtue in this realm and, thus, sociologically looking at it, one would find and can not but conclude that this phenomenon has developed the following characteristics:

a: That there is no human agency, human mind:soul:will but an 'automated', programmed and manipulated physiology, that does not think, that does not want to learn and process knowledge and information because they have their 'gadgets', 'devices' and contraptions' and the 'script' of 'behaviours, conducts and what and how to be in the distorteddia, to do that for them so that the entire basis of humanity being an agency of a human mind:soul:will has been taken down.

b: This is the pre-condition by which the foundation and pre-requisite technicalities are brought about to convert all physiologies into a mob. A mob is like animals in a stampede: animals as a mob in a stampede and humans as a mob both are the same in one fundamental way: neither think. They act in one goal: for humans this is programmed or orchestrated or brewed or manipulated but for animals it is not programmed by anyone but by their very fear and paranoia of losing their lives and in the process freezing in a state of utter and absolute panic and, thus, they run, often, to their deaths. So, this mob behaves the way it is programmed and it does not and can not behave any other way for the 'individual', that is a must requisite for thinking, considerate, thoughtful, learning, contemplating and developing mind or the agency of the mind, no longer is existent in this scenario. Only this individuality makes a human being unique and capable of running its own self and own agency. This has been 'terminated' from these distorteddia. This is why in that realm of the distorteddia people behave the way they do: they say anything, they do anything and they do not fall short of doing anything so that all the negative traits of dehumanisation: the lack of common human decency, kindness, respect, regard, care, empathy, solidarity, connectedness, communality and civility and social cordiality etc have been replaced by 'mechanistic' dehumanisations.

In this people are taken onto a 'state', where no one is being or doing but, simply, 'watching' or, rather, watching themselves, as well as, others, being and doing nothing. In this they neglect their own self, own health and well-being, their own environment and reality, their own individual life, their family life, their social life, the work, cultural and spiritual life. All have been 'connected' to this 'annihilation-machine', that, only, distorts, destroys, devastates, disconnects, disfigures, dismantles reality and humanity in that reality being individual, family, community and society and in this distorteddia do these: make a great deal of money, herd people, direct, dictate and manipulate people and impose its own 'set of agenda, priority and goals' into the population.

This is the most dangerous developmental stage humanity has reached and it has gone on to challenge, devastate and destroy the very basis of economics, politics, governance, public affairs management systems, rule of law and the delivery, conduct and running of the judiciary, as well as, destroying the learning, enquiring and innovating sense, space, spheres and culture, which have been brought to a point of, almost, a state of apology, for 'the god' of the distorteddia is utter, sheer and inescapable 'ignorance'. At the same time, seeking and searching for knowledge have been taken over by them as the direct route to 'dictate both what are searched for and what is 'made known' so that all this offers distorteddia to make more money and in this, valid, legitimate, professional, bona fide press and media and journalism, that are, absolutely and fundamentally, vital parts of a democratic society, governance system, judiciary and for social spheres and social and public discourse, have been, almost, killed off.

It is time the world, the world humanity, all the world's states and governments, all agencies of all shapes, sizes, manners, forms and types, as well as, every single human being on earth, in every country and in every nation, in every people and in every society, in every community, in every family must wake up, make a choice, make a stand up and fight this monstrosity of distorteddia and their utter, absolute and comprehensive devastating assaults on humanity by these machinations, by these dehumanisations.

While learning is a bio-intuitional cognition process, set by nature in all living organisms, on a scale of the lowest level and degree of sheer biological awareness to the highest level and degree of consciousness, that is capable of forming itself both as individual person and as a member of the unity of many persons or community or society and that is capable to cognise, combining both bio and intuitional in an alignment of all components of the faculty of rationality, by which, it thinks through and comes to cognition and that is learning and this learning is deposited in a 'bank', called, memory: from a single cell living organism with just biological awareness on biological cognition to a human brain:mind:will:soul with bio-intuitional cognition learning can and does take place. There is none and can not be any intelligence or learning outside living organisms, where we find things, matters, energies, time, space and void existing under absolute, incorporated, inherent and ingrained eternal natural laws without exceptions at all times, that not a single variable existing in it can alter or not obey, signifying there is no 'will' there, which does and can only arise out of intelligence through learning and all, that is outside the living-life, form part of what we call the Mechanoprincipium, which only the highest possible bio-intuitional intelligence, i.e, humanity is capable of perceiving.

Therefore, the very absurd ideas, that the misguided, manipulative and profiteering market mechanism of capitalism and all its distorteddia conglomerate are seeking to portray, establish, impose and dictate to humanity as artificial intelligence and machine learning are nothing but means to expand the scope, prowess and reach of dehumanisation and, must be, rejected, resisted, fought and defeated outright. We have, almost, more than half of all humanity and the great majority of women, forced and sentenced to live and die in no education, in desperate hunger, desperate poverty and abject poverty and malnutrition and without medical care, in homelessness and unemployment and much more besides and, yet, these forces are wasting all precious human and other priceless resources into such absolute and utter audacity of imposing their machinations on humanity, as, if, to suggest that for an injured soul dying in absolute agony of bleeding, hurts and pains the necessity is not to take her:him to the nearest accident and emergency unit of a hospital but get a plastic toy-robot-doctor to sit next to him speaking utter imbecility! This can not, should not and must not be let to succeed. The most vital and most scarce human resources must not be let to be squandered in this absurd and utterly misguided pursuit of dehumanisation for the purpose of making more profit faster and faster. Our high-most priority is to ensure that the entire humankind, in all nations on earth, is afforded the right to get an education and get universal human rights and not a single soul should die of hunger or for the lack of medicare.

This is what is called intelligence and this why it is called learning: because we are humans and we ask and raise questions and we empathise and we sympathise and we love and we hope and we imagine and we learn and we dream and we want to ensure our brothers and sisters and all our children are as valued, as safe, as protected, as respected and as nurtured as everyone else. This is called humanity and this arises out of this intelligence, that is an inalienable and inseparable part of the biological mechanism and architecture of life and, which, can not and does not exist outside this living-life and that mother nature has endowed each one of us with, when we arrive at our existence. Therefore, it is time for humanity to rise to reject, fight and defeat these attacks of ruthless dehumanisations by these concocted, brewed and miss-constructed ideas being sought to be implanted in our heads and minds by these distorteddia conglomerate of capitalism. This declaration invites humanity to reject the use of these concocted and brewed ideas and concepts of artificial intelligence and machine learning. We propose that, as part of the political and political economical fight against dehumanisation the world humanity adopts to reject these implanted terms and use, instead, machine processed programming:mpp for machine or artificial intelligence and programmed algorithmic machination:pam for machine learning, refusing the very concepts that machines can have intelligence and that they are, therefore, capable to learn. Likewise, we urge that the humanion adopst the use of the terms, self-driven or self-driving or autonomous vehicles for machines are not and can not be deemed to be having 'self', that absolutely applies to humans and autonomy applies to humans as individuals and as groups, societies, peoples, nations etc and can not be applied to machines. Therefore, auto-driven is the term we suggest for self-driven or self-driving or autonomous vehicles etc. This relates to profound, vital and fundamental issues and we must be careful as to how we use terminology, that, albeit, inadvertently, dehumanises humanity.

Against these distorteddia conglomerate, running a war against humanity, particularly, in seeking to destroy the human mind or the agency of the human mind, we turn to the human psyche. Imagine and, that what you do, becomes you for as soon as you imagine something it becomes real in your soul. And, here, resides the choice; even with imagination: what to imagine and what not to, what to become and what not to, what to do and what not to. Therefore, imagine love and harmony, joy and warmth, care and compassion, humanity and oneness, humanionship and respect, kindness and grace, togetherness and community, giving and expecting not to receive in return and selflessness and highest of wisdom; if, the world does not follow, your soul already has and, you are infinitely enriched by it already. Therefore, imagine! For humanics has set out the definition of humanity as an entity with infinite imagination, creativity and ingenuity and using all these infinities to the highest possible level and degree humanity becomes an infinity unfolding itself and, in doing so, humanics rejects and destroys the capitalistic prohibitive, restrictive and imprisoning paradigm of setting the possibilities, probabilities, capabilities of humanity, at a crippling level, which can be said as: 99% cases humanity is told: no, you can not do or be that and only in 01% cases humanity is told: yes, you can be or do that. Humanics puts forward the infinite prospects and possibilities of humanity. So, how does humanical psychology define humanity as souls or minds or wills. Psychology is the science, that studies and learns about the part of humanity, that we do not get to see: The Human Mind: Like the physiology, if, not looked after well, this human mind falters, breaks and falls ill for it needs 'food and nutrition', that do not come from physicality but are and can only be generated, in addition to keeping the physiology in a balanced state of good health and well-being, from and through being positively and actively engaged in the physical reality, created by family, networks of wider families, networks of friends, fellow learners, acquaintances and colleagues, networks of communities and the wider civic society: In short, healthy human mind is the statement, that says: There exists a civic society, that is capable of supporting, nurturing and sustaining happy, healthy and balanced human minds. So, what is the humanical formula in relation to a natural human mind: The less civic a society is the more mental and psychological damages it inflicts on all human minds, creating and sustaining the entire range of mental health issues. It can be seen as parallel to this sociological and political philosophical formula: A society, where there is hardly any rule of law, creates, sustains and maintains the highest degree, level and magnitude of repression, oppression, exploitation, violence, infringement, transgression, aggression, unrest, agitation, hostility, anger, animosity, suffering and injustices, all of which create and feed the conditions of the highest possible levels of all manners, forms and expressions of 'crimes' and such society simply ceases to be a society but becomes, effectively, a jingoistic jungle, in which all human minds are broken to destruction. There, in such a jingoistic jungle, therefore, can not exist happy, healthy, well-balanced human minds but the most severely destroyed, broken and devastated ones, that can not, ever, be 'mended' back to health. In other words, the closer the human mind is to natural justice the more it will be like itself and the farther it is away from natural justice the less it will be like itself and so far it is unlike itself is the part, that has been broken and, consequently, it has been made ill because of the breakage inflicted on it. Natural justice is what creates the conditions for natural humanity to exist and natural human mind is such a natural thing, that can not exist as it is, when dehumanisation breaks its home and takes it farther and farther away from its natural home, from natural justice, tearing it apart as it does so. But capitalism, with its enforcement of poverty and inequality, with all the high-cruelties, with all the dehumanisations, including, the dismantling, breakage, fragmentation, disconnection, isolation, disenfranchisement, disempowerment and dispossession capitalism advances a jingoistic political philosophy, with a jingoistic political economics all of which work to create a sociology of evil through creating a sociology of squalor, in which, all the qualities, states, straits, properties and characteristics of humanity are destroyed and in their voids all the negatives of these human qualities, that form the sociology of evil are sowed in. In such a horrendous sociological squalor thriving in the sociology of evil, the entire ecology is burning in toxic and lethal elements, that eat away anything human.

But a natural human individual lives and exists in many a unit of institutions, including, an immediate family, a wider network of a wider family, a core unit of friends, a social group of wider friends and acquaintances, a local community, a wider community and a society in general added to which because of recent development in technology the virtual reality. The most fundamental of all these are these three: the first being the immediate family, the second being the wider network of wider family and the third being the core unit of friends. Unless the individual is well connected to, with a to and fro active, engaged and positive relationship, with all these units and all their members, all of whom are active in the wider positive units, that spread outward, incorporating, all the basic units, than the individual will find it difficult to reach her:his full potentials and face the risks of all forms of shortfalls, including, illnesses of both physical and psychological nature. Unless an individual is seen as a metaphorical tree: that has two sets of roots, one, going up for light, air and space and another, going into the depth of the earth for other necessary goodness for life, without which the tree will struggle to survive, will stunt, decay and suffer as it does so until the end: than she:he is not seen as she:he is in 'potential' and this person will face the same fate as that tree, that lacks the two sets of roots. For humans, the first set of roots goes onto the earth of its core family unit, which is based on the earth of the wider units referred to and the other set of roots goes upwards to the wider units of society. With both these sets of roots the individual generates enough sustenance to support, foster, nurture, enhance, empower and create a personal eco-system to create her:his personhood, being, existence, where one is fully equipped to bring about all the potentials one has onto reality. Yet, capitalism, with all its distorteddia conglomerate and their dehumanisation war against humanity means that all these are dismantled into shreds and the persons are spread into a void of what once was or what could have been. This is how dehumanisation has devastated humanity and it keeps on doing so, now, with much more power, ferocity and speed because it now has the newer arsenal of the distorteddia conglomerate and because capitalism has been established across the earth as an unopposed system and with all its power to manipulate dehumanisation of humanity has been reaching to a point where humanity has now no other place go. Humanity now faces this wall and, unless, it fights back and defeats the monstrosities of capitalism humanity will perish as humanity naturale and will be replaced by the sociology of evil in sociological squalor, that will be occupied by only the physiologies of what once used to be called humanity.

Now we begin listing all the high-cruelties capitalism has developed, does deliver to the vast majority of humanity and that, it has established as features, that must-be-accepted and imposed on humanity for its system to keep going and it expects, demands and commands that all humanity accepts it without a word and it has the prowess to enforce it.

Capitalism's High-Cruelties

::: a ::: Life Sentence Without Education

The vast majority of human beings of this world are born with a life sentence of wasting the human existence without any education; they are born in places and countries where they will exist without ever setting foot at a school. They will exist without ever being able to read or write, without ever getting to know what life is, what they are made of and what they are capable of and what they can do and achieve. They will not ever know how to seek and claim their rights of all sorts. They will not know that it is up to them as to what kind of life and existence they want to create for themselves. They would not know who run their country or why. They would not get to develop themselves. They would take whatever is given to them: they would be treated by anyone whatever way they want to treat them. They would live and die in poverty and so long they live they will suffer away. In societies, that are chauvinistic, misogynistic, that fosters, festers and permeates all sorts of impositions and mind-framing so that they remain in line, they remain unquestioning, accepting, particularly, if, they are girls and women. They are born in poverty, they grow suffering hunger, they suffer malnutrition, they suffer severe and acute malnutrition. They suffer many illnesses, that they can not afford to treat. They will grow stunting and they will suffer all the consequences of stunting. They will keep on suffering till they die, young. A whole human existence, suffered through a life-sentence without education. That is the highest most cruelty, that any society could perform, dogmatically, systemically and systematically, culturally, politically, socially and political economically. This way they are directed to take part in 'democratic' exercises, where they are directed to vote whatever way is beneficial to the 'social orthodoxy'. They keep on perishing away suffering, in the process, they will have children born in the same poverty with the same fate with the same life sentences. These humanity, in their hundreds of millions, among the humankind, will never know what a magnificent thing this universe is, how awe-inspiring way universal laws are working in maintaining the bewildering complexities of the magnanimous universe, they would not know what history humanity has been passing through developing itself all the time. They would know any science, any mathematics, they would not get to experience the soul-bending experiences of creating for oneself, writing a poem, creating a piece of fine art work, reading a work of fiction, listening to music or creating a piece of music or understanding a scientific breakthrough. They would never get to know how great human beings were born in humankind throughout the history and how, they being great women or great men, changed the world for the better. They would not know how humanity developed the sciences and mathematics and physics and astronomy and cosmology and astrophysics, that, eventually, enabled humanity to cross the space to land on the moon or, go venturing further out into space, to Mars. They would not know how the French Revolution happened or what it did to the world. They would never know what October Revolution did to humankind. They would not know what the Long March was about. They would never know how our forebears crossed frontiers and along the way developed themselves and populated the earth. They would never know what Heraclitus said or Socrates did. They would never know what Helen Keller did or who she was. They would never know what Maria Sklodowska Curie did. They would never know what William Shakespeare did or Maya Angelou did or the fact that there was, once, a Martin Luther King, who fought to change America for the better. They are given the most horrid of all the sentences human systems can deliver: a life sentence without education. The highest most cruelty imposed on the vast multitude of humanity is imposed on them by this monstrous capitalistic system and no one has any reason to stand up and say: I want this system to be torn to dust so that it can not administer such barbaric a sentence on humanity any longer.

::: b ::: Life Sentence of Homelessness and Perpetual Persecution

Most people, regardless of whether they live in advanced, middle or low income countries, are, effectively, homeless, in the sense that they do not have a home of their own. In this, they live in other people's places and they pay rent all their life and this way they are persecuted out from one home to another all their life. In one life time, a family, may, move twenty, thirty, forty times. These people are supposed to be citizens of their countries, except without having a home, they remain cut out from the wealth of that nation and this group is the largest one in any nation. They have no home. And those, that have their own home, that they buy with a mortgage so that, effectively, their homes are owned by their banks. And, in this group, there are millions of families, who have bought their homes and their income is such that, after paying the mortgage and all other bills, they have hardly anything left to live and these people live in a hellish life of poverty. What makes their life even more miserable is this fact that, often, they have no money to do repair work of their house so that they are living in a place, that they can not fix so that it keeps on getting worse and worse and they are stuck in this hell of poverty-eaten misery of a life. And, then, there are people, who are homeless and floating away at bread and breakfast accommodations without a time limit. Their life, family life and their children's life and education, all are in limbo and they suffer from all forms of illnesses and negative impacts of all this floating about. They have no home nor do they have any hope of getting one. Then, there are many people, who are homeless and they are unable to find places to rent and, thus, are left on the streets and are living in the streets, rough sleeping and suffering away and dying away. The vast majority of the humanity of any nation are homeless and they remain homeless all their existence. This is the first and foremost disconnection between the people and the land they are supposed to belong to. Further, the people, individuals and families, that keep on being driven out from one home to the next, keep on moving and, this way, they simply, do not get to create and maintain long-standing connections and relationships with people where they are living, which impact on their mental health and well-being. They live somewhere, where they have no connections and it does not help that they are on their way to another place. This is a high cruelty, discharged to human beings by this capitalist system. This affects every human soul, particularly, the young ones so that they live but they really float and get floated away. This rootlessness causes endless sufferings to human souls and this creates communities as sand-grain-collectives, where humans living in a social and communal ecology do not have connections to each other or with anyone and they do not get to create and make and maintain such connections and relations because individual families of that collective keep on being moved elsewhere.

::: c ::: Life Sentence of Rough Sleeping

Capitalist system delivers this short and terminal sentence to the poor, who fall through from very many positions of life and find themselves on the streets. They suffer the ignominy and cruelty of seeking to live and exist on the streets and, keep on suffering and die away. Capitalism does not find it at all problematic. It is normal in capitalism that thousands and thousands of citizens of countries are sleeping rough in the streets and hundreds and hundreds are perishing away every year. If, this is not barbarity, if, this is not high cruelty, if, this is not brutal savagery, humanity ought to call in the hyenas and ask them to define what barbarity, cruelty and brutal savagery are! But this goes on in every capitalist county in the world. Humanics declares it barbarity, cruelty and brutal savagery and calls humanity rise to bring it to an end.

::: d ::: Life Sentence of Working Poverty

This is the most devastating of all other high-cruelties that in all capitalist countries, most working people are employed and paid, what is called minimum wage, which is the term to describe the lowest possible wage, that can be paid within the law. This means that capitalist countries, the most advanced to the least developed, it is legally allowed to pay the majority of the work force the lowest wage, with which no one can pay for all their necessities so that they work and, yet, they find they can not pay all their bills, that they still are keeping hungry or going half hungry. In places, where there are such charitable provisions, they go and line the food bank because they can not feed themselves with what they are paid. In some countries governments pay additional benefits to such workers, but since the financial crash all governments began drastic cuts to these benefits so that more and more people are going hungry and are lining the food banks, despite working! What is, even, more vicious is this fact that most of these low-wage-earning working poor people are families with young children and these children are sentenced to grow in poverty and suffer hunger and malnutrition and this does not bother anyone and political parties have programmes of 'austerity' for which they have no worry. They do not find it as a problem when elections come, their manipulation and propaganda will get them elected by these very people, whose live-in-life-sentence of misery they have delivered and will continue to deliver. This high-cruelty is devastating lives of many millions of families in all countries.

::: e ::: Life Sentence of Unemployment

At any given time at any nation there is and there is always going to be a per centage of the populace, who will remain unemployed, who will not find employment because the capitalist market economy can not create full one hundred per cent employment. Whatever the propagandists say or claim capitalism can not create one hundred per cent employment. This population ranges from single digit to double depending on what part of the world the country is in but regardless of the fluctuation a per centage of the working age population remains and will continue to remain unemployed. In countries where there is no social security protection, their life is a living-breathing sentence of misery and hardship and ignominy and they have no means of escaping it. They and their families must suffer the failures of the capitalist system, that can not create full employment. In countries where there is social security benefit the capitalist system and the states and governments use it as punishment tool and they punish people for being unemployed and despite these minimal benefits they keep on punishing these people and their families for not being employed. The benefit is not enough, however, so that it is, as, if, given to keep the person not dying of hunger so that these benefits sustain half-hungry and half-eating humans. They can not live nor can they die. This is the on-going and ever-going punishment protocol, designed and delivered by capitalism and its many states and governments to the unemployed poor.

::: f ::: Life Sentence of Unemployability

This life sentence of unemployability arises out of the people, who are born in families and communities, who have been cut out of development through education and training for generation after generation so that they are part of communities abandoned by the system where families have never received any kind of education and:or training so that they could get to better their condition of life. In such families no one has gone to college or university and their entire family and their network of families in such communities are on such social conditions, that they can not get any job because they have neither the knowledge nor the skills necessary for any job. They are, thus, made, unemployable. The only way the life condition and life chances of these people can be improved, is, if, there are great investments in these communities and all their members get to receive the benefits of education, training and learning so to acquire the necessary education, learning, training, skills and knowledge and development with which to seek employment or get into enterprise and business. But no government is committed to do anything with such communities. Further, the token mandatory education system keeps on producing a great number of the young people going through it as unemployable simply because they did not get to achieve the necessary literacy and numeracy required for people to be able to do the basic starting level jobs. These people are unemployable and remain so without any other initiatives being thought of or implemented to improve their lot in life. This group of people are literally left abandoned in the sociological squalor and they waste away in all forms and manners of negative and corrosive activities.

::: g ::: Life Sentence of Poverty

Poverty is created by capitalism simply because it lets the owners of the means of production to steal the majority of the value or worth created by the workers so that the owners pay as little as possible to workers as wage or salary by which the workers can not meet all their needs. Therefore, they suffer the consequences, that is poverty. Were there no stealing from the worth or value created by the workers there can not and does not exist poverty but, then, in such situation, capitalism can not exist for it must ensure the owners are able to profit from their investments, which they can do as and where they are able to steal a greater part of the workers' created worth or value. Thus, those, who receive an income despite creating much more worth or value, are demanded to suffer the consequences of their owners 'thefts'. This suffering of poverty appears in two different accounts: one account is the person's personal life, in which this person would suffer being unable to pay for all the items and things one needs for daily existence. They, may, pay all the bills and find that they do not have enough to buy necessary and nutritional food and drink so that they, might, end up eating less and drinking less of what they should have done to meet the physiological and nutritional needs of their bodies. Or they, might, buy cheap food and drink, that are not adequate for their needs but that's all they could pay for. Or that they, may, go half hungry or they, might, suffer from other cuts in necessity. They, might go and get some food and drink from the foodbanks. Generally, they and their children will suffer the consequences of being in poverty. But the second front of poverty is that sociological squalor, that is outside them and because they are poor, they will find that in that sociology of squalor they have hardly anything going: there is no service running or anything, that is running, is being run skeletally so that most of the services, that they would need are not there or these are skeletal so that it leaves their needs unmet or decimally met. Both these two fronts of poverty keep on devastating the people on poverty. This impacts harshest, hardest and strongest on the most vulnerable: the young, the elderly, the frail and the ill and all these groups are faced with this high-cruelty of capitalism, that they can not and do not get to escape and it keeps at tearing them apart till the end of their existence. The young being left to carry on suffering and passing the legacies of these sufferings to the next generations because a great deal of it gets translated into the physiology, biology, genetics and neuro-psychology.

::: h ::: Life Sentence of Hunger

Hunger is the absence of necessary foods and drinks, that human body and physiology require in order for it to function properly and run and maintain the physiology in good health and well-being or being able to create, sustain and maintain a state of homeostasis. These nutritional necessities are not given to the human physiology when people are left in poverty so that they either have no regular income or their income is lot lower than what they need to pay for the necessities. In this people go hungry and suffer the consequences. This is the highest and rawest form of cruelty, barbarity and brutality imposed and delivered to the poor of this humanity. This hunger can be full or it can be on and off or it can be perpetual in the sense that a person, may, eat little every day or every other day. In short, all hunger can be equated to nil nutrition to malnutrition to severe and acute malnutrition. Adults will and do suffer the consequences of these various types of lack of nutrition and they will get various illnesses but those, who are already suffering from various illnesses, those, who are old and frail, those, who are disabled and those, who are young and growing suffer the consequences of these lack of nutrition to the worst possible degree. But the most devastating of all the consequences of lack of nutrition or mal and severe and acute malnutrition are suffered by the youngest of humanity because these little humanity are growing and they can not grow well and naturally when they are suffering from the lack of necessary nutrients. This means that they do not grow or developed the way they should have and they stunt, as well as, developing many other developmental illnesses. They grow stunting and they grow shorter, leaner and thinner and they live shorter and die younger than their natural counterparts. This way a great number of human beings die unnecessarily and a great many human beings die young. And the consequences of these are passed from one generation to the next. This vicious, this brutal, this barbaric sentence of high-cruelty is acceptable and accepted and natural to capitalism. Humanics came into existence to eradicate this vicious brutal and inhuman barbarity out of this earth, out of reach of any human population.

::: i ::: Life Sentence of Malnutrition

This is a common form of suffering in the majority of the population of the world because most people are poor and most of them are eating and feeding their families and the young with very little nutrition, that are necessary for their bodies so that all of them suffer its consequences for most of their life and they develop many illnesses and a great many of them die as consequences to this continual suffering of malnutrition. The vast number of young, new-borns, babies, toddlers and infant perish away in their very young age because of these evils across the world. A great number of humanity, suffering from these cruelties in early life, grows stunted and continue suffering and die lot younger than other non-suffering humans.

::: j ::: Life Sentence of Destitution

In many countries in the world, even, in the advanced economies, various realities cause people to fall into destitution, in which they are abandoned to the elements. They find no refuge, no support, no help, no assistance; often, they are old and ill and infirm and frail and they are suffering from range of health conditions and they are left to fend for themselves buy begging and getting abused and maltreated in the process. This is natural in capitalism and it does not create any news.

::: k ::: Life Sentence of Social Security Benefits as Enforcing Punishment

In countries where there is social security benefit states and government use them to punish people for being poor or for being jobless. This is always used against people and, particularly, when governments want to support their rich masters more so that they seek to reduce the amount of money being paid to these poor people and having taken this money off the poor the governments, then, allocate and deliver these funds into the pockets of their rich masters. These governments and their states punish the poor and the jobless for being poor or for having no job while they know that capitalism can not create full employment so that there shall always remain a per centage of the total population as unemployed. However, these benefits are paid in such amount with which these people can not live properly. These benefits are paid to people in such a way, as, if, to ensure that they do not get to live fully while they do not die either. They are half-kept alive by keeping them away from half death. This is the absurd expression, that comes close to describe the nature of this horrendous benefit or social security system in capitalist economies, that is designed and delivered as punishment.

::: l ::: Life Sentence of Suffering in Illnesses Without Medical Care

In great many number of countries in the world there exists no universal health service so that the poor are left to fend for themselves, which means nothing other than that they fall ill and they continue to suffer till the end because they can not afford private medical care. This means that millions and millions of people, particularly, the young, the elderly, the frail, the infirm and the disabled suffer the most and millions die of easily treatable and preventable illnesses. This horrible state of affairs in the absence of universal and free healthcare is one of the biggest causes of millions of lives being lost every year. In this a great number of new and young mothers die giving birth and a great number of new-borns do not survive their first year of birth. And, this does not seem abnormal or unnatural under capitalism for you are poor and you die suffering: this is not and it does not make news in capitalism. If, you are rich, you must not die suffering from an illness, that you can treat with the highest paid physicians at the best equipped medical facilities in the world. This is capitalism: except the truth is: this poor is the worker, this worker is the only human in this world, that has the power to create value or worth while this rich person, who has billions, does not have this power and can not create a single cent or single penny of worth or value because this rich person is not a worker. But the rich have become rich because they have the lawful right to rob the workers' created worth or value and having been robbed off the workers are, then, asked to pay for the 'robbery' undertaken by the rich by serving a live-in-life-sentence in their own life while the rich live in decadence and abundance of absolute luxuries.

::: m ::: Life Sentence of Suffering in Desperation of Neglect Without Social Care

In in all countries, rich and poor, there either is no social care or whatever social care existed is now being cut to the bone so that everything is falling apart. The very people, who have given their entire life and life's work and energy into their nation, who are now vulnerable and unable to look after themselves while these capitalist societies, their states and governments are refusing to look after them. They are abandoning these very flesh and blood of everyone, who is working today, exactly the way these elderly people used to do but now their very governments and states are refusing to support and care for them. This is the biggest uncivilised and barbaric conduct of capitalism. It used these people and robbed their created worth and value all their working lives and now, they are being utterly vulnerable and helpless and capitalism says: go and fend for yourself! This is barbarity in action, that capitalism is. It is barbarity and brutality and viciousness in action every day and every night and always.

::: n ::: Life Sentence of Suffering in Horrendous Toxic Environment

This requires very little to be said about it. The entire natural and built environment has been made into a toxic mixture of volatility in terms of human health and well-being, particularly, in poor and developing and least developed countries but the advanced and rich countries are not without horrible environment. This horrendous environment is comprised of combined deterioration in the natural environment, built environment, in the waterways and rivers, canals and lakes and seas and oceans and in the air there are much damages and harms caused; everything put together, has created a formidable challenge to human existence and health and well-being, particularly, for the young, the elderly, the infirm, the ill and the disabled. They are paying the highest of prices in all these added harms through the toxic environment

::: o ::: Life Sentence of Suffering in Toxic Air Pollution

Air pollution has reached the most horrendous pollution level and become toxic and dangerous for human health. A great many number of human lives are lost as direct consequences of air pollution, particularly, the air pollution caused by the road traffic burning fossil fuel and the industrial pollution, particularly, the pollution caused by the burning of coal. But, again, the young, the elderly, the infirm and the disabled are paying the highest price as they suffer more from various illnesses, which get far more impacted by air pollution.

::: p ::: Life Sentence of Being Born and Dying in Millions

This relates to the world and the whole human race: if, one looks at a year, they have a spread sheet of how many millions of human beings and, how many, children died in that year and this figure would make an average nation of the current world. One looks at this figure and one wonders as to what kind of a kind or species one belongs to, this kind, called, humankind, which the brutal and barbaric capitalism has dehumanised to such an extent that it is, increasingly, becoming neither human nor kind. What kind of a kind this humanity is that it does not even blink when each year almost the equivalent of an average nation disappears from the earth as deads from various causes, most of which are preventable and all of which arise out of capitalistic barbaric brutalities. These brutalities happen and can happen because capitalism ensures that the world is not united under one unity of a body, that has the duties, obligations and responsibilities to work to protect the world as one and protect, safeguard and advance the interest of this one world's one and only resident, one and only citizen, this humanity, this entire humanion. And because of this capitalism goes on as the killing mechanism, to keep on killing and mauling and terminating human beings in their millions every year as the vast majority of humans keep on serving their live-in-life-sentence of continual suffering of hardship, misery, agony and pains. But this The Humanics Elleesium Declaration 2019 declares its end: capitalism has done its killing long enough; it is time to put it in a coffin and put it in the vault of the museum of sociology for posterity. It is time for humanity to take forward ourselves towards a humanical society where no one dies unnaturally. Meaning every human life exists naturally and comes to its end as nature brings it to an end without any other causes or factors shortening or cutting abruptly short that human existence.

Therefore, we arrive at The Humanics Elleesium Declaration 2019 call humanity to rise to seek to make humanity as one in a world as one, in this one Sunnara, in this one Milky Way Galaxy, on this one whole Mother Universana, on the path and course of seeking to reach humanics, which begins with the setting up of a Universal Assembly of Humanity, it is a Mother of All States, Governments and Human Public Affairs Management Systems. It is an impossibly difficult, painful and heart-wrenching time, that the world and the humanion are faced with today. If, one takes a look at a space of, say, last twenty years, than, one would find that the world has been progressively becoming a more dangerous, more lawless and more jungle-like place. International law has become an obsolete phrase. It is literally the law now: save yourself. However, it all started with the collapse of the old Soviet Union, that, suddenly, put the world's existing, albeit, tension-strewn equilibrium into a hole where it simply got lost and disarrayed. United Nations began to become weaker and weaker, in which process, the USA, for some impossible reasons, began to show the tendency that it could take over the world policing so declared George Bush to make the United Nations an 'irrelevant body', which is what happened to the United Nations. Effectively, this world body, that acted as the main source and origin of international law, despite being a weakly construction, has been made into a 'dinosaur' organisation. However, the recent events across the globe, that are taking place at this very moment, should establish the following facts, loud and clear:

A: That the United States or any other individual government no matter which it is, can not replace United Nations.
B: That the United States simply can not act nor can it organise, assert or impose its will to the world or any other particular nation. Nor can any other state or government, such as, Russia or China or India or Britain.
C: That the world continues to become more and more dangerous and lawless unless there is a Universal Body for the whole Humanion is here to foster, support, promote, work for and guide and lead the world towards law, order, equality and fairness between and among peoples.
D: That the European Union alone can not deal with any of the sudden problems of migrants:refugees, that are now threatening its borders:security etc.
E: That all the major issues of today, that we face in this world: trafficking of humans, children, women, migrants, refugees, illegal weapons, drugs, medicine and human organ business, servitude and slavery of a myriad of types, manners and forms, maltreatment, abuse and exploitation of migrant workers, state-sponsored slavery, inequality between and among humans, inequality between genders, violations of human rights, wars, famines, states being non-existent, as well as, all infrastructures being crushed, lawlessness, violence, rule of power:might:arms by groups bringing anarchy, no support network, criminals taking up challenging the entire so-called legal bodies, including, the states, piracy, abduction, murders, robbery, rapes, violence and maltreatment and subjugation of minorities, poverty, lack of education, lack of housing, lack of employment, lack of medication, lack of all provisions, lack of support for the vulnerable, such as, the elderly and people with disabilities, conditions and states, that are essential for life, living and human dignity are disappearing, cruelty, brutality, barbarism and bestiality in the manner in which these expressions of evils or anti-humanity is exercised, perpetrated and promoted, inequality in trade and commerce, inequality and unfairness in the global business arena, giant corporations, though, legal in countries where they operate, becoming

more powerful than even states and, thus, dictating terms of reference in whatever fields they operate on, Apple, Google, Yahoo, Facebook, Amazon etc and more, so that people are simply shepherded into their prowess, the United States is enjoying the benefits of simply having its currency dollar becoming a by default or pseudo world currency while the world could, should, ought to and must have an international currency of its own, the national economies, such as, China, India, Brazil and more are becoming so huge that should they go downhill the entire human economic and financial structures, might, come undone in which case there is no world body, that would be there to help humanity not to fall into a dark night of anarchy and suffering. In short, this is an immediate list of our troubles.

The United Nations seems to have had its day like the League of Nations. It is now high, high, high time that the entire Earth, the Entire Humanion have a new agency, An Assembly of the Humanion, equivalent to a state, of the entire Humanion with its jurisdiction covering the entire human race, the entire earth and the space and beyond and all the nations and states are within its structures so that everyone follows its laws. The humanion is analogous to a human physiology in which we have individual cells working together whereby similar cells coming together making tissues, which, in turn, get together and form muscles, that in turn, form organs, that, in turn, form systems, that, in turn, work together under the guidance, leadership and wisdom of the mind and brain. The Humanion is such an entity where each individual human is such a cell and all of us make the body of the Humanion. We can not exist singly and our moral imperative is to work jointly, together, in unison so to ensure that the individual could exist, live and prosper doing the same for the whole while the whole exists to ensure all the singularities of its members are supported, fostered and empowered.

Such an organisation can be truly called The Universal Assembly of the Humanion, over which there is no one: those, who believe in God, over it is God and those, who do not, over it is humanity in general. There is not, can not be, shall not be, ought not be, must not be any force. Force does not form part of humanity but rationality and the choice of the free, which are to guide us within the framework of laws and reason. So long we are involved in wars and physically fighting each other, exploiting each other, subjugating each other, depriving each other, forcing each other, dominating each other, prohibiting each other, letting a lot of us live and die in hunger, in homelessness, in malnutrition, in joblessness, in illiteracy, in lack of medicine and provisions, that are essential for human lives we must treat ourselves as UNCIVILISED that we have so far failed to make ourselves civilised for children are dying of malnutrition, women are being bought and sold and trafficked around the world, people are dying of preventable illnesses while there is medicine for it. Our sole aim, must, therefore, be to CIVILISE ourselves. Get humanity out of this inhumanity into a true civilisation, that can only be achieved by humanity when we reach and establish humanical societies on earth under the rule of law in natural justice, setting free all humans into liberty and equality at all times.

The Universal Assembly of the Humanion is the rightful body to be able to command and establish its will, which is the will of the Humanion, over the people it is designed to assert itself over: asserting means asserting the rule of law and the due process of law. And to set it up we must go back to the drawing board and forget about the old-fashioned way of looking at things. Imperial powers, colonial powers, first, second and third estate or the rest must be abandoned for no big power can solve the problems and challenges the human race is facing today, tomorrow or the day after simply because we have made a mess of our human affairs management system because we have let this killing mechanism capitalism to bring us to the destructions, devastations and ruins of dehumanisation, establishing the reign of terror of poverty, distributing the anarchy of inequalities and enforcing the barbarity and viciousness of all forms of high-cruelties on and over humanity all over the earth. If, they can not solve these problems and challenges themselves than they should just abandon the old-dated, failed politics, the dead-duck political philosophy and the dysfunctional and anti-nature, anti-rationality political economics and the world and world humanity must start afresh.

There is no qualitative difference between, the Maltese as a nation and the Chinese as one, number is a quantity not quality. There is no particular qualitative difference between America and France or Germany and Russia. All the humans, that form these nations are simply the same humanity, albeit, speaking different human tongues, that operate by the same reason and ration, which human brain does, who are simply placed at different parts of the earth but each and every nation is comprised of the same humanity, except, each is geo-located on a specific space and place on earth or they are geo-located but they are and they remain so: humanity. Each nation of the humanion gets a seat at the Assembly and there is no such thing as veto power. It must be established on a democratic philosophical base, structure, footing, ethos and culture.

Structures of the Universal Assembly of the Humanion: This Assembly is comprised of A: The Universal Assembly; B: The House of the Guardians: The Upper House; C: The House of Nations: The Lower House; D: The Humanion Exchequer House; E: The House of Judiciary.

This body is truly a Universal Government, which shall have moral, as well as, political, we would call it humanical and judicial authority for the fact that members were elected in various ways and those, who are predetermined are so by virtue of their specialism, in which they have already spent their entire life in specific field. There is no membership fee for the members of the Assembly. No member state pays any membership fees other than donating twenty per cent of their national forces, i.e, their law enforcement force, their armed force, their naval force and their air force and any other specialist forces to the Assembly so that the Assembly on its day of inception has an 'Armed Force' in all appearance, ready at its command, that are situated at every corner of the earth, to enforce its will against any nation or country, that stands opposed to the 'Will' of humanity, a will, that arises out of nothing else other than a democratic, lawful and valid course of deliverance in pursuance of the due process of conducting the law of the Constituted Universal Assembly of the Humanion. This Universal state and government would have its own source of money because it has its own Central Bank and this body will create, run and manage that currency, which will be the International Currency for the Entire Humanion and the entire world to use.

This is the body, that the progressive political forces, newer humanical political forces and movement, that are very likely to develop from the international movement of the sector comprised of the social enterprises, that has been developing all over the world, the not for profit agencies, community interest companies, charity organisations, voluntary and community groups and organisations and other such similar agencies and co-operatives, that run themselves without seeking to make profits for their owners and shareholders, must, work together as international forces, united in one purpose and aim: to bring the world and world humanity under a truly democratic, equitable and just framework of governance: under this Universal Assembly of the Humanion. These newly re-arranged and newly-formed political parties and forces create a new political movement around the world and they should work to create conditions in each country and nation so that they present and promote and run a learning culture of political philosophy, political economics and jurisprudence among their members and to the wider public, from whom they are seeking to get members and voters to support their political programmes. In this these political forces run a 'political university', for their members and for the public and from there they create political awareness and make the people taking part in these learning activities more aware, more focussed and more determined in continuing the work to make better the human condition.

These new political movement across the globe will work in all countries and nations but form the architecture of the entire world's political forces in a grid, whereby, together as the world entity, world movement, they subscribe to the formation, bringing into existence this Universal Assembly of the Humanion as a whole, which, can be summarised as: seeking to establish the mechanism to bring the world under the rule of law in natural justice where the entire humanity acts and works and exists as one while accepting as the yardstick of conduct, behaviour, act and work: that each and every nation of the humanion are of equal worth, status, dignity, value and respect and all nations must be afforded equitable and fair treatment and respect at all times. Everyone as individual humans is equal to everyone else while all nations and countries are equals among the assembly of equals. This world body establishes itself as the body-originating: the governance structure, the executive, the trade, finance, fiscal and business, the legislature, the judiciary and all the supplementary systems and mechanisms, including, a central bank and a currency of its own, which is to be the world's currency of trade, commerce and business. The rest of the world's states, governments and bodies fall in their respective places onto this grid of international governance and public affairs management system architecture and the world works and exists as one, in which, the humanion works and exists as one. There does not appear or remain interests contradictory between the interest of the Assembly and any individual national interest since the interest of a geo-located humanity, a nation's, can not be contradictory to the interest of the whole humanity since the interest of the heart in a human physiology is inherently not and can not be contradictory to the human physiology's interest to create, sustain and maintain homeostasis in the physiology for without the state of homeostasis being achieved he heart simply can not function as a proper heart nor can the physiology work properly, if, the heart does not function properly in support of its seeking and achieving homeostasis.

In the national arenas these political forces and parties will work to create the broadest possible platform in the basis that the entire people of a nation is divided into two opposing camps: one, in their tiniest minority, the rich, who own the vast parts and segments of the wealth, assets, properties and all the means of productions of a nation and the other, the vast multitude of all other people, who are workers: that we define, as any person, who works and gets paid a wage or salary or who gets an income from a work, that she:he has created, who are called self-employed, for their work and these people do not own much in relation to the individual worth of any average member of the rich club. This means that these political parties are essentially workers parties, except, workers are not defined as Karl Marx had sought to define them. All humans other than those, who are rich and who take profits, dividends and othe rewards, payments and packages of advantages, facilities and provisions from the entities by virtue of their owning them are workers. Those, who buy shares in companies, which are minimal and minuscule in size, who work and who continue to sustain and maintain their existence by the wage or salary they earn are workers, too. Therefore, in humanical definition the vast, vast majority of humanity are workers, in this an artist, who happened to become rich because, she:he has suddenly become very 'fashionable' and her:his works sold and made her:him rich is still a worker so long she:he stays or remains rich this way. Were they to invest their riches and begin taking the 'benefits' from them as the rich do she:he will join the rich club and cease to be worker other than the specific time, in which she:he works as an artist, creating something, when they should be treated as worker. Humanical definition of worker relates to humanity and the human elemental qualities: that a human being uses her:his infinite imagination, creativity and ingenuity to create products, services and provisions, that have inherent worth or value ingrained in them and that, they bear and contain the quality or property in them, that make them able to meet human utilities. In this the employment of these three human qualities or states in the quantity of infinity, imagination, creativity and ingenuity is the yardstick to assess whether someone is a worker. A teacher is a worker, an engineer is a worker, a doctor or consultant is a worker, a person working at a Café or a Supermarket is a worker, a driver of a train, a nurse, a solicitor, a social worker, an office worker, all are workers. The only people among humanity are not workers are those, who get to make and receive a whole lot of money every year because they own things and they receive the 'benefits' of these ownerships, rewards, profits, bonus, dividends and other payments without any other qualification, other than the fact that they own these for which they get benefits out of them.

Now these new political forces will create a political programme of actions, that has a dual-stage approach in which they seek to work to create a 'Pre-humanical' society by bringing capitalism under the absolute control and jurisdiction of the rule of law, within their national economies with a clear and corresponding re-arrangements in the world's governance mechanism so that capitalism begins to fall in every country, one after another, under the absolute control of the rule of law and jurisdiction. In this state of pre-humanical phase of human development and progress these political forces will seek to create a situation whereby capitalism is run under the rule of law and the laws are crafted in such a way that the market is re-created and re-designed to bring the entire functional and functioning mechanism of capitalism under the rule of law so that every political economical entity in a country exists to serve the people, the nation and the country and they do not exist to serve their owners or shareholders as primary beneficiaries. It is still capitalism and there is still ownership and owners and shareholders still own and still make and receive profits and benefits from their ownerships but the entire nation's GDP, first, serves the entire needs of the nation and, then, the rest goes to pay for the cost and count of profits and who gets how much is decided.

These political parties will strive and work together in unison with the similar forces active across the world in all countries to bring about the emergency and existence of the Universal Assembly, which will not happen unless and until countries, one by one, begin the transformation of capitalism into Kapitalawnomics, which is the state, where capitalism is made to function under the rule of law, that makes it work and exist to serve the human condition, the country, the people, the nation, the humanity of any nation. As the countries in the world increase in number, which have gone to these new political forces, that have been converting capitalism into Kapitalawnomcs, more countries will find inspiration from them and more will follow the same course and the movement to establish this new Universal Assembly will grow stronger and stronger as more people will begin to join the movement and, eventually, the new emerging and inspiring group of nations, running Kapitalawnomics will join forces and lead and establish this Assembly, which will inspire the rest of the world to follow this new, lawful, peaceful and democratic revolution of leading the entire humanity and the entire world towards the path of pre-humanical societies, which then will work together to reach and establish humanical societies in human enterprise.

In this stage of pre-humanical society, these new political forces and parties seek to eradicate all the high cruelties, that capitalism distributes among the vast majority of humanity. This state is called Kapitalawnomics, whereby capitalism is run and conducted under the rule of law. This phase will eradicate poverty and inequality by removing capitalism's ability to distribute and enforce high-cruelties, all of which will be eradicated by the introduction of the building-block foundational human rights. Overnight, these high-cruelties will disappear and, though, inequality will continue to exist, so long this money-based system exists, it will be reduced to the minimum possible state and it will not get to increase for the base-line of the cause of these inequalities will have been removed. Because without foundational human rights in existence existing human rights are useless for most humans on earth.

In our works on Humanics in all three volumes, as well as, four volumes of our work, 'Dehumanisation of Humanity' and our other relevant works, 'Sociology of Evil', 'Psychology of Zoohuman' and 'Alphansum Sovereign Necessarius', some of which have not yet been fully published, have, together, presented all these various parts and components of the entire way towards humanics. The Foundational Human Rights are the Foundation on which all other human rights, including, the ones accepted in the current international laws but, most of them are, simply and utterly, hypothetical and non-existent, because of the political philosophy and political economics run in the world. The building-block foundational human rights will exist and enforced and established and citizens will have the legal pathways to ensure their enforceability or challenge their infringements or violations in the court of law. Without these Building-Block Foundational Human Rights the existing human rights are 'worthless and nothing but glorified' declarations, that, in most parts of the world, are utterly non-existent and where there are claims that they are followed are not true either because of many other desperate states, including, poverty, homelessness and lack of rights to have access to nutritional food and drink and right to degree-level education and many other things. The Guaranteed Universal Income in Humanics is not anything, that has so far been proposed by many thinkers and, in some places, there are tinkering going on. Humanics-proposed Universal Income is derived in altogether different way than taxation or national insurance and it creates the conditions to end poverty, end hunger, establish the conditions to fulfil the right to nutritional food and drink, bring about equality as close as is possible within a money-based system before humanity reaches towards humanics, giving every single citizen of a nation a genuine, verifiable, measurable and legally enforceable stake to the entire wealth of that nation and all this goes towards supporting all other Foundational Human Rights being achieved for all members of a particular society.

The Building-Block Foundational Human Rights are
A: Absolute Right to Live in Clean, Healthy, Safe and Natural Environment
B: Absolute Right to Breathe Natural, Fresh, Clean and Safe Air
C: Absolute Right to Necessary Nutritional Balanced Food and Drink
D: Absolute Right to Free Medical Care at the Point of Need
E: Absolute Right to an Absolute Home
F: Absolute Right to Free Degree-Level Education and Life Long Learning
G: Absolute Right to Guaranteed Social Care:
H: Absolute Right to a Universal Income
I: Absolute Right to a Job
J: Absolute Right to Dignified Civic and Human Funeral Paid Through by Universal Income

Once these building-block foundational human rights are established and delivered to each and every single citizen of a country it will create an astonishing civic society, that has no parallel in human history. This phase of pre-humanical society and its work in preparing the pathways towards humanical society will create the conditions, in which the not for profit sector, social enterprise sector, ownership social, community interest company sector, charity, voluntary and community sector and the co-operative sector of the economy will develop rapidly and, initially, begin to increase its total output to the GDP and soon this sector will take over the 'owned' part of the economy in terms of their combined economic output and, further, through the collapse of the established 'brands and bodies' of large companies will continue to grow and more and more of these entities will fall away from realities of communities, where a new movement of communities will arise to create infrastructures to replace these disappeared and disappearing 'brands and bodies', which will be owned by no one other than these entities serving and belonging to their local communities. All these new areas and types of in-prospect humanical entities, will soon take over and lead the economy in terms of their combined economic outputs and in that stage of the development of the pre-humanical society, the communities and society will be able to create small versions of human enterprises, which will begin to show what and how human enterprises look like and are run and how they can be created and operated. This phase will continue so that in a short space of time now, the majority of economic output is created by social enterprises and the owned part of the economy will keep on decreasing in size and influence and another mechanism will begin in which the pre-humanical in-prospect human enterprises will begin to convert into human enterprises increasing and supporting the new added impetus of newer and faster growth of human enterprises. There will arise a time when the entire society will create pre-humanical in-prospect humanical economics bodies, that create the entirety of the economic output by itself and the owned part simply will have come to cease to exist. In this stage the society will be poised to create the humanical society where more than half of the entire produce of products, services and provisions of society are created by humanical human enterprises while the rest are produced by pre-humanical in-prospect human enterprises, that will continue to convert into human enterprises as time moves on with the humanical development. At this state and stage of pre-humanical development of society Kapitalawnomics will become the mechanism, to enable these fast and tremendous growth and vibrancy of the humanical spirits of society and all the conditions of a humanical society will have been created and a country, a nation and a people can move into creating and ushering in humanical society without any form or manner of any kind of upheaval or disturbance and, Kapitalawnomics will have earned some accolade to add next to the monstrosities capitalism had created and distributed and with these capitalism will have been silently buried into the sociological history dustbin without anyone shedding a tear for its demise nor there will be a single newspaper in the world, which will publish any news about that silent demise and discarding of capitalism, the killing mechanism and the delivery vehicle of monstrosities of dehumanisations and high-cruelties, brutal barbarities, vicious and violent savagery to humankind. This is a revolution, for the first time, in the human progression, that is bloodless and peaceful. It is an unbelievable reality and vision, that humanity will be capable of being able to attempt and deliver a revolution, that will change the destiny and condition of the entire human race forever without any disturbance, any bloodshed or any destruction of life. Because one can not aspire to deliver justice with bloody hands: a civic society, a humanical society, that aspires to bring about the rule of law in natural justice, establishing humanity at equality and at liberty, eradicating ownership and money and setting all humanity free towards eternal learning can not do so were it to invite humans to hatred and bloodshed. Humanics shows that humanical societies are the most civilised architecture, that humanity will be able to create because humanics makes humanity to believe in this simple infinite source of power and force: humanity is an infinity unfolding itself. Humanics, in a humanical society, is where humanity literally does unfold itself as an infinity. It is a long walk, to humanics, but the world and the world humanity must not fail in taking this road and keep on walking towards the shores of the joys of humanics.

Back to this society, which has neither structure nor shape nor there are dignitaries, such as, President or Chair or Prime Minister or Chancellor; it is, therefore, as open, as shapeless but as real as the Universe itself, which contains everything and enables their very existence within the bounds of its own laws, that are invisibly at work without fail. The Universe can simply be seen as the expression of liberty and so can society be seen as mirroring this. From that liberty of the Universe and Society we seek the laws, that set the perimeter of that expression of liberty, which concerns humanity so that we find the shape, size and contents of equality and, then, go about seeking to achieve that equality for without equality liberty does and can not exist. And because we have not achieved equality we find all societies in the world are doing nothing but bleeding for the wounded liberty and, thus, gasping equality with it because it can not be. One can not exist without the other: if, one is hurt both bleed. In ordinary everyday terms: liberty and equality can be said as being: soul-mates. Or the other way to look at liberty and equality is to say: no one can say where neurology begins and ends and cardiology ends or begins for both reach and cover the entire physiology: Liberty and Equality are like that so that it is impossible to separate them; neither can live alone nor separately. They are one as two or two as one. The purpose of sociology is to bring them both to life in one as one as two or two as one. The purpose of sociology is to bring them both to life: liberty and equality so that both exist equally, one being the other or being one together and in them humanity finds its home at homeostasis, which is now, thus, made of natural justice, where purpose and meaning are planted and harvested, through human endeavours of creativity, imagination, ingenuity and work. This is the humanical sociology's vision of a humanical society.

Imagine, a tiny village in the wide expanse of a valley of a mountain, that overlooks two countries on its either side beneath, almost, an infinite sky, hanging down with a display of wonderful skyscapes: open fields and valleys, rivers and lakes, hills and groves, marking the map with nature's bounties. Through that tiny village go parallel a high way and a railway line, linking the wider world to the village, stopping at the tiny railway station with white sign boards marking the station, that is lamped with old Victorian lanterns. There is the station office and there is a tiny cafeteria, served by a very old man of, almost, 90. There is a primary school, secondary school, which feed into colleges and universities, that are in the wider world, two small markets, connected to the wider market and its chain, a mosque, a temple, a church, a pagoda, a synagogue, linked and connected to the wider spheres of faiths. There are playing fields, farmlands, where people are living and going about their business of life. All this is connected to this: social interactions of people, among and between them, through established rules and customs and through and by organisations, institutions and structures, that they have developed to support them in living life, which is to be able to imagine, create and live. To be useful to others, as well as, oneself and one's family and community. So, the Station Master sells tickets, the Station Porter goes up and lights up those old Victorian Lanterns at dusk and puts them off when the trains stop for the day, the old man, who did not have to work still gets up at three o'clock in the morning to open his café, which his family asks him to stop doing but he does so that the people for the early dawn train would find warmth and can have a drink, the Doctor goes about seeing her patients, the Chemist goes about offering medications to people, the religious persons go about doing their parts in the 'temples' mentioned, the primary and secondary school teachers go about teaching, the farmers and fishing-folks go about farming and fishing, the cafes and restaurants go about serving people, the social, political and cultural spheres work on.

The study of all this is to understand how this network of people and organisations and the culture, that they help create work, develop and run on and this study is the domain of sociology, which means it can not be done properly unless it has an eye in the depth of understanding the political, economical and jurisprudential philosophy and the management systems, that they have created, that go towards creating and enabling that culture to which Sociology tries to offer its lights. On a humanical perspective sociology is a tool to understand the inner striving of humanity to create peace and stability, through which, life is supported, enabled and nurtured, which means to achieve natural justice, liberty and equality for only which establishe the due process of law, in which the rule of law is the 'nature' of society and the people, who live in it being purposeful and useful to wider life while being able to support and develop their own, being at liberty, being at equality and protected by the same laws, that protect everyone else equally and at all times.

And in this vision of humanics in this humanical society, for the first time in the development of human condition, is able to create a its own 'voice' as organisations, such as, the state and government, legislature and judiciary, by taking them through a metamorphosis and re-casting, re-creating, re-organising and re-orientating them into new entities, which are so, because society has been able to develop all its citizens into highly educated, highly developed and highly equipped intelligence, highly sophisticated minds with continual and eternal learning and development driving them forward and further, who run them through the direct form of democracy, humanicsovics and the entire nature of the entire mechanism of public affairs management system is transformed, that exists as the society does: to continue to be a civic society, that illustrates how equality and liberty look like at a functioning level and field of reality in practice under the rule of law in natural justice, where humanity is an infinity unfolding itself through the highest usage of its infinite imagination, creativity and ingenuity. That infinity of humanity as humanity-naturale is released and let free in this humanical society, that is conducting itself in human enterprise.

And, having this beautiful vision of humanics in mind, imagine: take the entire universe off existence: you can imagine this but there, must, still, exist this I and this you to imagine the universe away into non-existence. And, this I, this you, can not imagine the universe off existence without being in existence. The question is what kind of existence is that, then, when the universe is imagined away into non-existence: the physical and temporal part of this I and this you can not exist, if, the universe and her temporal framework do not exist: or, rather, unless we imagine our temporality into non-existence we can not imagine the universe into non-existence. So, how do this I and this you exist in that 'state', where nothing temporal exists: these two entities, therefore, can only do so in the non-temporal a state. And what is this non-temporal state. Alphansum is the non-temporal: the eternal and the infinite: therefore, imagination is the only thing, that takes humanity to the state to reach, empathise and understand the 'state of Alphansum' and, there, this I and this you, find, see and empathise the existence of Alphansum and, thereby, their own existence outside temporality: that 'existence' of Alphansum is described as isz: that, what always isz: not being or existing but, simply, just, isz and isz outside temporality. This is not 'existing' in the temporal but isz in infiniternity with no beginning middle or end for, only, time and space or the temporal, has a beginning, middle and end. Therefore, Alphansum isz: therefore, I isz and exist in both infiniternal and temporal and, thus, this I and this you, are and can not but be an infinity unfolding itself, through imagination following the nine-step-realm-path: if, Alphansum is the truth the entire creation and the universe are that truth's beauty's Eden Garden, expressed in the infinity of its expositions, magnificence, brilliance, artistry, sciences, mathematics and creativity, all of which unfold by the laws of the Mechanoprincipium, so that the entire Universe and creation are the true nursery of liberty and equality in natural justice existing and unfolding in the rule of law and, in this scheme of things, humanity is the custodian of the eternal learning of the Mechanoprincipium and with the enlightenment, gained from it, to seek and try to become and unfold that infinity, called, humanity with the full utilisation of the infinite imagination, ingenuity and creativity.

In our search, in reaching the Mechanoprincipium, we find the temporal Universe, that exists, enabling all things and entities of all kinds, including, time and space, all of which abide by and exist in the continual and eternal following and observance of the Universal Laws, enshrined in the Mechanoprincipium, we find that humanity as an infinity unfolding itself can not but have a home exactly as this Universe, which we termed as Universana. There is one humanity and there is one home for this one humanity: this Universana. Now, this Universana follows the Laws of the Mechanoprincipium at all times, so we see that, our human rationality has the structure, mechanism, system, processes and complexities, architectured in a layered-up and stratified way so that there are many layers, placed one over the other and all are structured in a proportional continuum both towards the most small going inwards or towards the largest going outward and in this reality, we find are contained all realities: the human natural reality, that contains in a gated, closed up physiology, the many types of realities, all of which keep on getting smaller and smaller and all of them are rising towards reaching the mammoth seismic and all of which, take us back to the Mechanoprincipium, that our human rationality is a nano-compressed, individualised nano-crosm of the Mechanoprincipium and this human rationality follows the laws of that nano-mechanoprincipium at all times, eternally, like the entire Universe following the Universal Laws of the Mechanoprincipium at all times. Therefore, we can not but accept that we humanity must do the same: that we learn and develop ourselves in such a manner, that is pre-requisite for us to be able to do so, about these nano-mechanoprincipium and the Mechanoprincipium so that we are able to exist and live by the Universal Laws of this set of Mechanoprincipiums. This is how we derive at our aim, our goal, our objective, our philosophical and moral imperative of seeking to establish a society, that is civic, that can not be so, unless and until we reach to the stage and state so to be able create a humanical society, that runs and conducts itself under the rule of law in the due process of the law, in natural justice and in such a humanical society humanity is let free in equality and at liberty so that the human society stands to directly reflect, mirror and resonate the Universana whereby both entities, the humanity and the Universe are now always guided and led by the same Universal Laws of the Mechanoprincipium. How do we know that there is such a thing, Mechanoprincipium: the very creation, development and continual progression and continual new emergence of new branches of science, knowledge and learning, of all the branches of learning and knowledge, sciences, mathematics, medicine, engineering and all other humanical branches of disciplines of learning show us that there exist the laws, about which we are beginning to learn more and more and the more we learn the more we see that the entire 'sphere' of 'wisdom' or the light or the entire knowledge-sphere is organised in an infinite grid of learning, where laws and learning and wisdom are ingrained. The more we keep on learning, the more we know and the more we are capable of seeing more of this infinite grid, illuminating.

This grid of learning or knowledge or wisdom shows us the fact that the shores of the Mechanoprincipium are always and eternally lit by the light of the laws, that govern the Garden of Eden of this Universe. This is why we, humanity, must be, eternal learners and we must keep on learning and developing ourselves so that the more we advance in our learning the better we are able to follow these magnificent Universal Laws and, by being able to continue to do so, we keep on advancing and taking forward and making better the human condition on earth, on the Sunnara, in the Milky Way Galaxy, in the Universana perpetually. With eternal learning with eternally developing humanity we keep on developing for with having only less than three percent of our human genome being expressed so far, a conservative estimation of time and length and stages of development for the human genome to be expressed by its entirety, by 100%, would be to say that it will, probably, take another four hundred million years for humanity to keep on developing so to be able to reach young adult stage of development! Because now, we humanity, is literally like a crawling baby, making a mess of things across the earth and see what a mess we have made and continue to make. This hypothesis of humanity needing another four hundred million years of continual and progressive development to reach young adulthood is compatible with this astronomical fact: that the Sun, in our home-county, the Sunnara, will continue to burn for another eight hundred billion years! Therefore, humanity will have been going and learning and developing for a very, very, very long time and in that long continual development humanity will keep on getting better and wiser and more capable and the more capable and the more wise we get the more we become able to keep on taking forward and keep on advancing our human condition so that our society will continue to grow more humanical and more civic as it gets closer and closer towards following the rule of law of the Mechanoprincipium. Capitalism, therefore, is the most imbecile, most idiosyncratic, most absurd, most anti-nature, most irrational and most horrid of anything else, that has been created by humanity. In this, capitalism is nothing but a killing mechanism, that punishes the vast majority of humanity with desperate cruelty of poverty and the miserable inequalities with all the brutal, vicious and barbaric high-cruelties it creates, distributes and enforces. It is time humanity stands up and say to those, who want to show that capitalism is the high pinnacle of all human development: it is anything but that.

But this walk to humanics is a long walk. Human enterprise is the political economical system of a humanical society, in which no one owns anything but everyone belongs to the whole as the whole belongs to everyone lawfully and equally and, it neither believes in nor makes money but human utilities, needs, aspirations, creativity, imagination and dreams are served without money, where everyone works and creates for others as others create and work for them, thus, bringing in meaning and purpose to life, along with it come natural justice, equality and liberty, that establish a true civilisation.

But until humanity has achieved the conditions to fully discard capitalism and put it in the archives of history of human development and begin to craft humanics, capitalism must be brought under, run and managed by the rule of law and the absolute yardstick of that law, must be, that it, must, always, serve the entire people of a country:nation. Capitalism can not, as it stands, nor can it be modified to do so, so long it remains a system of money to make profits, deliver 100% employment. Never can it deliver this. Thus, societies can not 'punish' the poor, the working poor and the jobless, the elderly, the frail, the ill and the disabled people nor can it punish children and young people in desperate poverty, hunger, malnutrition and suffering, who are part of this society and who are placed in such vulnerable conditions because of the innate nature of the capitalist system to create, distribute, sustain and increase poverty and inequality.

Therefore, all the new and progressive political forces, this new wave of political movement across the world, will be initiated and led by the youth of humanity, must seek to advance a political programme as part of their political determination to bring capitalism under the rule of law so to convert it into Kapitalawnomics and in this new political programme they, must, include the initiation and materialisation of the Building-Block Foundational Human Rights.

So, long scenes like these, in which human souls are treated with such brutal, barbaric, cruel and absolutely dehumanised, demeaning and ruthless degradation and contempt, abandoned to suffer and perish away on the cruel and cold streets, homeless and sleeping rough, humanity can not claim that it has learnt the 'C' of Civilisation. And the forces, groups, people and political parties, that do not see this as to how horribly, terribly, dangerously counterproductive all this is to a society and to human progress and, added to this denial, they continue to advance, support and maintain this horror of a punishing doctrine of sentencing people to suffer this wasting away of human existence must be taken on by these new and progressive humanical political forces and fought on and defeated because the vast majority of people are in this horrendous state and they can not and will not accept this horror, once, they are made politically aware, politically educated and politically conscious about the mechanism and system of this brutal barbarity, called, capitalism. And, this is why, these new political forces and movement, must, begin to establish and deliver through this 'Spartacus University of the Dispossessed', where they will bring in the mass of people to study and learn about the political philosophy, political economics and the sociology of torture, delivered by the capitalistic mechanism of killing and slaughter. These Spartacus Universities of the Dispossessed, will be opened across a country, wherever, there are people, in community settings, in work places, in villages and in towns and every space and place, where people gather and get the people involved through real life activities of learning and developing and connecting as individual human beings, supporting a regeneration, renewal and revival of human bond and kinship, that act as a nurturing, sustaining, enabling and inspiring source of infinite riches. This will serve two ends at the same time: this will ensure that the capitalist propaganda, directing, herding and manipulation do not succeed in blinding people but, at the same time, it will create awareness and consciousness among these people, to reject the extremist, xenophobic, racist and supremacist, religious and otherwise, violent groups and the neo-nazis and neo-fascists to advance their horrendous, reactionary and anti-nature and anti-reason monstrosities through vile, gross and crass nationalism, that fester in hatred, that feed and support the continual maintenance of the sociological squalor and the sociology of evil.

The current human condition is like society has deliberately stabbed majority of its members with terminal blows and now, letting them bleed, suffer in agony of pain and infection and die a lingering, slow-poisoned-death without any care being shown to them and society simply dehumanises itself as it does all humanity so that it is able to look at all these agony, strife, pain and suffering and pretends that it does not see. But this won't be accepted by the multitude of humanity, the workers of the world, who are the majority of humanity, once, the humanical forces begin to work and set out to establish this renaissance of learning and open their endless Victorian lanterns across the campuses in the communities, in the ever-expanding network of the Spartacus University of the Dispossessed. At the moment the neo-nazis, the neo-fascists and all other obnoxious and reactionary forces are using and abusing the dispossessed and feeding them with the toxic mix of raw, crass and base nationalism and xenophobia and racism and all other forms of prejudice, inflamed by conspiracy theories, malicious lies, dangerous falsehoods, concocted fabrications and invented mythologies, fuelled further by opinion fascism and sharpened into a deadly cocktail of hatred, anger, hostility, viciousness and animosity towards invented and targeted enemies, except, in all these the misguided populace are lost for their lot's misery, agony and dispossession are not caused by anything, that they are manipulated, directed and herded to claim to have done but the very capitalism and all its apparatus, that have sentenced them with this live-in-life-sentence of agony, misery , pain, hardship and suffering. They, will now, have the means to find another source, to get the real truth as to how and why capitalism has devastated their lives and how the status quo manipulates them and directs and herds them and gets them to vote for the elite again and again, the very elite, who will keep on ensuring that their live-in-life-sentence does not end and keeps on getting harsher, harder and heavier and longer. Political education, political economical awareness and sociological insight will clear the fog out and away from the eyes of the dispossessed and they will become knowledgeable to be able to see and rise and, then, they are the majority, whom, now, no political propaganda or herding could direct to act against their very own interests. And this massive but woken up and aware vast majority of the dispossessed will rise for the vision of humanics and human enterprise and for liberty and equality and they will tear away the card-castle of capitalism with peaceful, lawful and democratic a revolution, that the world has never seen in the entire of the human existence. This revolution is the humanics revolution: peaceful, lawful, democratic and natural for the rule of law in natural justice to go forward bringing capitalism under the rule of law first and use it to develop human society through the realisation of building-block foundational human rights, ending all the high-cruelties, including, poverty, hunger, homelessness and malnutrition and no education, that capitalism enforces into creating the conditions to enable humanity to usher in humanical society in human enterprise.

The Humanics Elleesium Declaration 2019 calls on all humanity, all workers of all humanity across the world, who are the vast majority of the world, particularly, the youth of the entire world to rise to challenge, fight and defeat dehumanisation and end all the monstrosities, high-cruelties and all forms, types and manners of poverty, that the killing mechanism of capitalism sentences the vast majority of humanity with a live-in-life-sentence of suffering, hardship, agony, misery and pain. This killing mechanism and punishment apparatus capitalism, that ensure that a handful of rich in each nation take hostage the entire nation and dictate and enforce a horrendous state of suffering to them can not go on any longer because it stands as a giant of a dead mountain, blocking the path of human progression, human existence and in the process it is killing humanity physically, as well as, through its dehumanisation and it has made human existence and human life for the vast majority of humanity on earth a miserable, horrendous and brutal punishment of agony, suffering, hardship and pain. It is time to begin this renaissance of revival, regeneration and renewal of the working people through a new learning revolution, initiated, led and run by new humanical humanicsxian political forces, led by the youth of the world, through which the masks and manipulations of the capitalism's propaganda and manipulation tools are taken off so that the killing mechanism is seen in its true features and with this new liberating and inspiring pathways to learning and empowerment about the political philosophy, political economics, dehumanisation, sociology, jurisprudence and other vital socio-political issues and the workings and apparatus of capitalism the working people will become more politically aware, more conscious more alive and more alert and all of which will inspire them towards uniting and becoming a determined political force to initiate and bring about the end of capitalism and usher in a humanical society.

Time it is for the youth of the world to take up the leadership to inspire and show the way to all working humanity towards a humanical society, existing in human enterprise, where all humans are set free at liberty and equality on the path of eternal learning and eternal development under the rule of law in natural justice where humanity is literally an infinity unfolding itself. Let the world, lead and inspire the world and world's working humanity to let free the eternal and infinite phoenix of eternal learning at the ever-increasing number of campuses across the globe of the new Spartacus University of the Dispossessed to initiate and begin a renaissance of learning, of empowerment, of re-enfranchisement, of re-empowerment, of re-humanisation, of reconnection, of renewal, of revival and of resurgence of the power of the love of learning, of human bond, of human kinship, of human connection and of our diversity unifying and our oneness strengthening the humanionship and unleashing, releasing and freeing us into letting free the infinities of our infinite imagination, creativity and ingenuity: the vast majority of humanity's working people are the dispossessed, who are now in possession and belongingship of the most impossible, most astonishing, most awe-inspiring, most empowering, the most liberating wealth of all worth and all value: the key of eternal learning to open and access and utilise to the fullest the infinities of our humanity's infinite imagination, creativity and ingenuity with which to unfold ourselves as the infinity, that we are, that we can be and that we can do: in human enterprise, in humanical societies, under the rule of law, in natural justice, being equals and at liberty, on the eternal path of eternal learning and eternal and continual development and progression.

Munayem Mayenin
April 06: 2019
London

The Humanics Elleesium Declaration 2019

The Humanicsxian Manifesto

The Humanics Elleesium Declaration 2019

The Humanicsxian Manifesto

Munayem Mayenin, London, United Kingdom

ISBN: 978-0-244-76474-6

Copyrights @ Munayem Mayenin, London, UK

First Published: April 06: 2019

Price: £05.00

An Imsonium Book